C000024966

The
Macmillan Way

A 235-mile Long-Distance Footpath across Limestone England

This book and the footpath it describes are dedicated to the memory of Douglas Macmillan MBE, founder of the organisation now known as Cancer Relief Macmillan Fund

CONTENTS

INTRODUCTORY SECTION   Page

   Introducing the Macmillan Way   2
   How to use this Guide   4
   The Macmillan Way Planner   5
   Walk Macmillan - Support Macmillan   5
   Cancer Relief Macmillan Fund   6
   The Country Code   7

CHAPTERS

1 Oakham to Flore   Maps 1 - 7   43 miles   8

2 Flore to Warmington   Maps 8 - 11   22 miles   22

3 Warmington to Maugersbury, near Stow-on-the-Wold   Maps 12 - 16   24 miles   30

4 Maugersbury to the Tunnel House Inn, near Coates   Maps 17 - 21   26 miles   40

5 The Tunnel House Inn to Bradford-on-Avon   Maps 22 - 28   37 miles   50

6 Bradford-on-Avon to Bruton   Maps 29 - 34   32 miles   64

7 Bruton to Abbotsbury   Maps 35 - 44   51 miles   76

   Index   96

   Acknowledgements   Inside Back Cover

Based upon the Ordnance Survey mapping with the permission of the Controller of Her Majesty's Stationery Office, © Crown copyright

Published by
The Macmillan Way Association,
St Mary's Barn, Pillerton Priors,
Warwick CV35 0PG

© The Macmillan Way Association

ISBN   0 9526851 0 8

Front Cover Photograph:
Ditchedge Lane - Page 34

Printed and bound in Great Britain by
J B Offset Printers (Marks Tey) Limited
Colchester, Essex.

Introducing the Macmillan Way

This 235-mile Long Distance Path has been developed to increase public awareness of the Cancer Relief Macmillan Fund and to assist in the raising of further funds for this vitally important charitable organisation, whose role is to improve the lives of people with cancer and their families.

In view of this, anyone walking all or part of the Macmillan Way can feel that they are walking *'Across Country for Cancer Care'*, as our waymark logo proudly proclaims. But at the same time they will be following a further, more geographical, theme as our trail has been planned to follow, as near as possible, the course of the long, oolitic limestone belt, which comprises stone known as 'Cotswold' in the Cotswold area, but which runs in slightly varying forms all the way from South Yorkshire to Dorset. The Macmillan Way starts from Oakham, rather than South Yorkshire, as the Wolds Way and the Viking Way already follow the oolite, down to this point. From Oakham it heads south and west to Abbotsbury in Dorset, a coastal village noted, like Oakham, for its lovely old limestone buildings. Here then is Macmillan Way's unifying theme - a succession of delightful towns and villages, almost all of which are characterised by their warm, toffee- or honey-coloured stone, and all of which are set in gentle, typically English countryside.

Like most long-distance paths, the Macmillan Way follows existing footpaths, bridleways and byways, and small stretches of minor roads when these are unavoidable. At times it shares its route with short lengths of a number of Regional Paths, such as the Leicestershire Round, Northamptonshire's Jurassic Way and Warwickshire's Centenary Way and with much of South Somerset's Leland Trail, but for most of its length it is an entirely new route. It provides a link in an existing chain of long-distance paths running from North Yorkshire to Oakham - the Cleveland Way, the Wolds Way and the Viking Way. It also links with the head of the Thames Path near Cirencester and with the South-West Coast Path at Abbotsbury. But perhaps the outstanding feature of the Macmillan Way is the rolling pastoral English countryside through which it passes - great tracts of quiet, unspoilt farmland, with views to distant skylines inviting the walker to go ever onwards. These farmlands are punctuated by great woodlands and secret, sunken paths overhung by trees, much as they must have been in medieval times. River banks and tree-shaded streams are often followed and hedges, many still not too ruthlessly trimmed, are usually alive with birds and small animals. No great climbs are required but when the flatter, rolling country ends, steep slopes lead up to ridge-tops from whence there are splendid panoramas ahead.

Our route sets out from Oakham, across the hilly Rutland countryside, before passing into slightly lower Leicestershire. It soon drops down to cross the Welland Valley into greatly under-valued Northamptonshire. After running southwards over quiet farmland and along a disused railway line, it passes Cottesbrooke Hall, the fine gardens of Holdenby House and the great Althorp Park, before dropping down to Flore in the Nene Valley. Here it crosses M1, the still busy A5, Watling Street and the Grand Union Canal before climbing gently onto the beautifully broad Northamptonshire uplands. Through a number of simple, unspoilt villages, past Canons Ashby House, and over old railway lines to wide-greened Chipping Warden. Now briefly into Oxfordshire and across the lovely Oxford Canal before heading into still-leafy Warwickshire, soon passing elegant Farnborough Hall with its grassy terrace overlooking a once quiet valley now disturbed by the busy M40. Climb beyond this up onto the scarp that soon runs into Edge Hill, with its views westwards over the battlefield and the Vale of Red Horse to the distant Malverns. Here the Way passes close to Upton House, with its attractive sloping gardens and outstanding art collection.

Back briefly once again into Oxfordshire, with its toffee-coloured ironstone and a real flavour of the Cotswolds. Along Ditchedge Lane, an ancient green road with fine views, and then down into the Stour Valley and through woodlands before climbing up into the true Cotswolds beyond Long Compton. Across high wold country, not far from the prehistoric Rollright Stones and past lovely Chastleton House before descending into the broad Evenlode Valley, with its memories of Jane Austen and Edward Thomas. Now in Gloucestershire, we climb once more up onto the wolds to pass close to historic Stow-on-the-Wold before descending into the Windrush Valley, to go through ever-popular Lower Slaughter.

From here we pass through many miles of classic Cotswold country, over high wolds and through a number of small villages, passing Chedworth Roman Villa before skirting the great Cirencester Park. Beyond this we go through great woodlands to emerge close to the old Thames and Severn Canal and the nearby source of the River Thames - the start of another Long Distance Path. Now west and south, over slightly flatter wold country, passing to the north of Tetbury before walking right through the lovely Westonbirt Arboretum.

We now head southwards into quiet Wiltshire farming country, the peace of which is eventually much disturbed by yet another motorway - the M4. But soon beyond this we start to follow the richly wooded By Brook Valley, first going through Castle Combe, once described as England's most beautiful village. We keep close to the By Brook as far as elegant Box, a village made famous by Brunel, who drove a long tunnel through its hill for his Great Western Railway. From Box we climb up onto higher country before dropping down into Bath's most elegant small neighbour, Bradford-on-Avon, with its fine old buildings including a unique little Saxon church. From here we follow the Kennet and Avon Canal for a mile or two, before heading southwards up the Frome Valley, passing into Somerset beyond the exquisite manor house of Iford and the rugged castle of Farleigh Hungerford just beyond. On down the Frome Valley before heading westwards towards the eastern Mendips, to skirt around busy Frome in a wide semi-circle.

We go down a deep wooded combe to Nunney's elegant castle and over flatter country at the head of the Frome Valley, before climbing up onto the ridge clad with the great woodlands of the Somerset and Stourhead estates. From Alfred's Tower, towards the southern end of this ridge, having perhaps first strayed from our route by walking down to Stourhead Gardens, we follow the Leland Trail, heading due west along an old road over flat country to the two delightful towns of Bruton and Castle Cary, both associated with Douglas Macmillan. We now climb out of Castle Cary, then through North Cadbury, across the busy A303 and below the great hill fort of Cadbury Castle, one of the legendary sites of King Arthur's *Camelot*. In hilly country to the south of Cadbury Castle we pass into our last county - Dorset - soon finding ourselves in the delightful old town of Sherborne, with its great abbey and two castles. From Sherborne our route passes through undramatic farming country - Hardy's *Vale of the Little Dairies* - at the centre of which is little, stone-built Yetminster. However, this is soon left behind and we pass through the great park of Melbury before reaching the delightful village of Evershot.

From Evershot we walk southwards to Cattistock, on Dorset's River Frome. We follow this southwards to Maiden Newton before veering slightly east to enter chalk country for a mile or two, thus briefly deserting our limestone belt. In consequence we encounter beautiful open downland country and only return to the limestone within a mile or so of the sea at Abbotsbury, where old limestone quarries are clearly visible from our pathway above the village. And so, to St Catherine's Chapel, on its hill above the village and the final walk down to Chesil Beach beyond.

How to Use this Guide

This guide to the 235-mile-long Macmillan Way is in two parts: The first, an introductory section giving some of the background to its creation and use. The second, a detailed description of the Way itself, divided into seven chapters, varying in length according to the appropriate stopping and starting points. The Key Map inside the front cover shows the way in which these chapters are split and which map numbers are covered in each chapter.

Each of the 44 double-page spreads is entirely self-contained, with map, text and possible illustration all inter-relating. This will ensure that when the book is opened out and inserted into a transparent map case, it can stay there until the next map section is reached. The maps are at a scale of 1:50,000 (about one-and-a-quarter inches to the mile) and are based upon the Ordnance Survey's Landranger series. The sheet numbers of the Ordnance Survey's Landranger and Pathfinder maps covering the area similar to that covered by each of our own maps are also noted. The symbols and conventional signs used on the maps are explained in the block below.

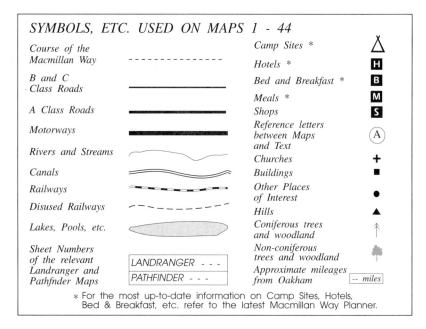

Each paragraph of text starts with a reference letter and this cross-refers with the same letter on the accompanying map. All information not concerned with the main Macmillan Way route is shown in italics, while the route details themselves are in normal type. It will also be noted that progressive mileages from Oakham are clearly displayed on every map and this will allow users to work out very simply the distance between any two points. It will also enable users to see how far they have gone and, by subtracting from the magic total of 235, to work out how far they are away from Abbotsbury. Perhaps this calculation should be avoided in the opening stages !

The 44 maps show the location of hotels, bed and breakfasts and meal places, either indicating their presence by being appended to the name of the appropriate town or village, or if well outside any town or village, their exact location. Details of these facilities are constantly changing and are not therefore included in this guide. However they will be found in the supplementary guide - *The Macmillan Way Planner*, which is updated annually, and details of which are shown below.

With the help of information in this book it should be possible to follow the Macmillan Way without further guidance. However, by March 1996, the route from Oakham to Abbotsbury should also be waymarked, apart from sections using public roads and at one or two points where landowners have not been prepared to have our waymarks on their property. The waymarks are of two types - a self-contained plastic roundel with arrow and Macmillan Way logo, and a self-adhesive sticker with Macmillan Way logo, which is stuck on a standard yellow or blue waymark arrow (yellow for footpath and blue for bridleway). We hope that you have no difficulties, but if any are encountered it would be appreciated if you could let us have the details - *The Macmillan Way Association, St Mary's Barn, Pillerton Priors, Warwick CV35 0PG.* This will help us maintain the existing trail and improve it where necessary.

The Macmillan Way Planner

It will be noted that, apart from symbols on the maps, there is no information regarding accomodation in this guidebook. These details have been omitted as they date so quickly, but they are available in the frequently up-dated supplementary guide, *The Macmillan Way Planner*.

Amongst other items, this includes details relating to: Hotels, B&Bs, camping sites, pubs and restaurants on the route, bus and train services connecting with the route, and Tourist Information Centres on or near the route. It also lists the towns and villages on the route and the mileages between them, the relevant Ordnance Survey Landranger and Pathfinder Maps and Route Directions and maps showing the diversion into Cirencester from Map 20.

The Planner is available from the *Macmillan Way Association, at St Mary's Barn, Pillerton Priors, Warwick CV35 0PG.* Please send a cheque or postal order for a minimum of two pounds, all of which will be passed on to the Cancer Relief Macmillan Fund (if you wish to send more it would be gratefully received!).

Walk Macmillan - Support Macmillan

The Macmillan Way has been developed as a tribute to Douglas Macmillan, the founder of the organisation now known as Cancer Relief Macmillan Fund and we are hoping that it will be used by a number of people who derive the particular pleasure known only to those who walk across country. If you haven't tried it yet - now is the time!

We are also hoping that the Macmillan Way will help to raise funds for the Cancer Relief Macmillan Fund and with this in mind, might we suggest that you 'sponsor' yourselves for a small sum per mile and ask your friends and relations to help out by also becoming your sponsors. When you have finished your walk **(either the whole route or, more likely, part of it)** we should like to send you a Certificate of Congratulations. Could you let us have a cheque or postal-order (made out to *The Macmillan Way Association)* for a minimum of one pound to cover costs. However if you have managed to collect some sponsorship money (either from yourself, or from your friends and relations), this would be gratefully acknowledged on your Certificate. It is also hoped to be able offer badges too, and details of these will be sent with your certificate.

Congratulations on completing the Macmillan Way, **or that section of it which you planned to complete**. Do let us have your comments , both on the Way itself, and on the way we are organising it. They would be very welcome. Letters to: *The Macmillan Way Association, St Mary's Barn, Pillerton Priors, Warwick CV35 0PG.*

The Cancer Relief Macmillan Fund

This organisation owes its existence to the vision of one man, Douglas Macmillan. Shocked by the painful and distressing death of his father in 1911, he saw that little was being done for people with cancer. His concept - *that by improving the knowledge of cancer amongst the public and amongst health professionals, the needs of cancer patients would be better understood and their quality of life improved* - remains as true now as it was in Douglas Macmillan's day. Everything Cancer Relief does is directed towards improving the care and support available to people with cancer and their families.

This national charity has pioneered many new initiatives including specialist cancer care centres, information services and Macmillan doctors. But, of all its work, The Cancer Relief Macmillan Fund is perhaps best known for its funding of Macmillan cancer care nurses, trained specialists in helping patients fight cancer - with more than medicine.

Macmillan Nurses - specialists in cancer care, working with doctors and nurses to support patients through treatment

There are now more than 1,300 Macmillan Nurses offering expert advice, pain and symptom control and emotional support to people with cancer and also their families. They are based all over the UK and work as part of the NHS, sharing their skills with medical and nursing colleagues to help raise the standard of cancer care generally.

We hope that the Macmillan Way will serve to increase public awareness of The Cancer Relief Macmillan Fund and also provide some financial aid, however modest. So, please give your support. One in three people develop cancer at some point in their life, so directly or indirectly, it affects us all.

Walkers will be interested to note that Douglas Macmillan was born and grew up in Castle Cary and at one time walked daily to school in neighbouring Bruton. Both towns are on the course of the Macmillan Way and young Douglas must have followed at least part of our route on his way to and from school.

The Macmillan Way is dedicated to the memory of Douglas Macmillan MBE, whose clan motto is, most appropriately, `I learn to succour the distressed'.

The Country Code

Enjoy the countryside and respect its life and work - **Guard against all risk of fire** - **Fasten all gates** - **Keep your dogs under close control** - *keeping them on leads when there is any chance of encountering stock. Don't forget that pregnant ewes are very much at risk even from merely playful dogs* - **Keep to public paths across farmland** *and walk in single file to minimise path-spread or crop damage* - **Use gates and stiles to cross fences, hedges and walls** - **Leave livestock, crops and machinery alone** - **Take your litter home** *(nice thought)*, *but if you are some days away from home, dump it in a litter bin in the next village you pass through. Don't forget that litter is not only untidy, but it can also cause great harm to animals and farm machinery* - **Help to keep all water clean** - **Make no unnecessary noise** - **Protect wildlife, plants and trees** - **Take special care on country roads**, *usually walk towards oncoming traffic, but on blind bends walk on the outside of the bend where you will be most visible (we have tried to minimise the use of dangerous roads, but there are a few stretches which require great care).*

A Friendly Countryside for All

While planning the Macmillan Way we have received great kindness from many land owners and tenant farmers and we have assured them that walkers along our path will go quietly through their land and that you will not give offence. If you look at things from country people's point of view, they are far more likely to appreciate yours.

When meeting anyone on your journey, take time to stop and pass the time of day with them. Many farmers and farm workers to whom we have talked, say how surprised they are by the number of walkers who just plod by without even saying hello. Stop to talk and you could well learn so much more about the country through which you are passing. Don't be discouraged if you don't always get a response, but keep trying - the overall result will be well worthwhile, and the next Macmillan Way walkers that come along are more likely to have a friendly welcome. We have all got to live together, so please - let co-operation be your watchword, rather than confrontation, We are sure that you won't regret it.

Track beyond Little Brington (see page 20)

7

Chapter 1   Oakham - Flore   43 Miles

No doubt you will be anxious to start on your journey, but do try to spare an hour or two to look round Oakham, once England's smallest county town and still the administrative centre of the old county of Rutland. See especially the unique collection of outsize horseshoes in the 12th-century Castle Hall which is situated within the earthworks of the long vanished castle. See also the delightful 17th-century Buttercross and the slender spired parish church, the interior of which includes a fascinating series of carved arcade capitals. If time allows do try to visit the most interesting Rutland County Museum in Catmos Street.

Situated at the centre of the town, the Library and Tourist Information Centre stands not only at the start of the Macmillan Way, but also at the southern end of the 140-mile Viking Way down from the Humber and at the western end of the 100-mile Hereward Way across from Thetford. Our own route from Oakham as far as Belton-in-Rutland also follows the same course as the Leicestershire County Council's Leighfield Way.

(A) Start walk from Library and cross road before going down Mill Street (SP - *Brooke*). Mill Street soon becomes Brooke Road leading south-westwards out of Oakham. Over railway-crossing with care and turn left immediately beyond, continuing on Brooke Road (SP - *Brooke*). Leave Oakham by primary school on right and start to climb road up hill. *Views of Rutland Water, England's largest lowland reservoir, over to left.*

(B) Turn left off road near top of hill just before small wood on left, and along track with hedges on both sides. Pleasant views down to right. Turn right, through gate where green road comes in from left and start going down into valley keeping to immediate right of hedge-line. Under power-line, through metal gate and second metal gate just beyond small mound on right. Continue down between two hedge-lines which get closer as we descend. Join smoother track by cottage on right and over old stone bridge crossing River Gwash. Pass Bridge Farm on right at entry to small village of Brooke, joining road and soon pass church on left. *Do not miss a visit to Brooke church, one of the most attractive churches on the whole route. It has a squat 13th-century tower and an exceptionally interesting and unspoilt interior including old stone floors, box pews, screens to both aisles and a fine 17th-century tomb.*

The 17th-century Buttercross, Oakham

(C) Soon turn left at junction (SP - *Ridlington*) keeping on road out of valley with wide verges and young trees. Turn right at x-rds (SP - *Braunston*) keeping on road past Shorne Hill and Hibbits Lodge on left

(D) Turn left (SP - *Leigh Field Lodge*) onto still surfaced road and soon between stone gate pillars with Prior's Coppice over to right.

Just before cottage on left pass entry on right to Prior's Coppice Nature Reserve. Go between second pair of stone gate pillars and onto bridleway (SP - *Leighfield Way*) passing farm buildings on left and starting to drop down to valley with fine views ahead.

(E) Bear left keeping on track to left of Leigh Lodge farm buildings and the fine old stone house of Leigh Lodge. Earthworks of old fish ponds on both sides of track immediately before bridge crossing little River Chater. Climb out of valley on well surfaced track and eventually go between third pair of stone gate pillars by large barns on right.

(F) Turn left at junction of tracks just beyond barn and almost immediately turn right at

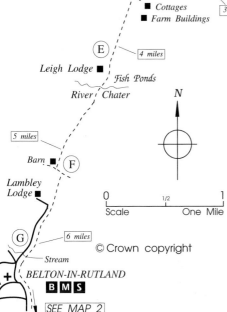

MAP 1

LANDRANGER 141

PATHFINDER 896

second junction. Now start to drop down rough track into valley with hedge to right. Track improves as it is joined by track coming in from right from Lambley Lodge and then becomes surfaced road.

(G) Over small bridge crossing stream and climb hill into attractive stone village of Belton-in-Rutland. Bear left at x-rds into Chapel Street with its attractive ironstone cottages (SP - Allexton) and bear left into Nether Street by war memorial, with church up to right (but turn right if you wish to visit Post Office Stores, the Sun Inn, or The Old Rectory). *The large church has an impressive tower with gargoyles and a spacious interior with stout sandstone arcading, an interesting font and a handsome 18th century wall monument.*

9

(A) Bear left down hill to leave Belton-in-Rutland. *(From Belton to Hallaton we share paths with the Leicestershire Round, a 100-mile circular walk around Leicestershire.)* Over the busy A47 **with great care** and continue on minor road to cross Eye Brook by Bridge House (once a mill). We now leave Rutland for undisputed Leicestershire and enter Allexton village. Go straight, not left at road junction, and up road with old rectory and church on left. *The church, in an overgrown churchyard, has a medieval tower, but most of the rest dates from the 19th century.* Bear left before reaching entrance gates ahead, keeping on road. Pass through pretty village green and at end go to right of last house on left *(Innisfree)*. Up short, narrow path between overhanging bushes. At end of path, over fence, turn right and keep to immediate left of hedge-line until almost reaching gate at end of field. Good view of Allexton Hall down to right.

(B) Now bear half-left up hill to cut across corner of field towards electric pole. Over stile half-way up fence-line and head down across large field aiming just to left of house on horizon (*Allexton Lodge*) and, when they come into view, just to right of two trees. Over stile and small bridge and across second field, still aiming to left of Allexton Lodge. Go through gap in hedge and still aim for left-hand end of Allexton Lodge. On reaching stile in fence, do not cross it but note diversion of path along fence line to right. Now keep to right of Allexton Lodge.

(C) Turn left at end of fence and follow to right of fence up hill. Fine view back over valley of the Eye Brook to Belton-in-Rutland church tower. Now pass to right of Allexton Lodge and soon turn right to follow down to immediate right of hedge-line. At end of hedge go through gap between hedge and fence coming in from right and go straight across very small field heading slightly left towards small gate. Through gate and down field towards gap in hedge. Through gap and aim for right of Fearn Farm's buildings. Over stile and go left along farm track for a few yards to Fearn Farmhouse.

(D) Turn right, opposite farmhouse (SP - *Hallaton*) and through three metal gates, keeping to immediate left of hedge line. Over stile and then through metal gate. Go down field continuing to follow to left of hedge-line, with fine views ahead over rolling countryside to distant Northamptonshire skylines. Over double stile at bottom of field and head straight across large field on same line as hedge previously followed, aiming just to right of left-hand of two old railway bridges. Cross small bridge over stream and bear slightly left to left-hand of two railway bridges. Over this bridge crossing disused railway and over stile just beyond. Over fence and then keep to its immediate right for short distance. Over stile in left-hand corner of field

and go diagonally across large field aiming for signpost at road junction, with building to its left. Over small bridge about two-thirds across field, crossing small stream and soon through gate onto road at junction.

(E) Keep in same direction down road (SP - *Hallaton*) passing sports pavilion on left

Unusual Market Cross at Hallaton

10

and soon enter delightful village of Hallaton. Pass large duck-pond and Fox Inn on left. Well beyond Fox Inn bear right at junction (SP - *Cranoe*) passing attractive thatched cottages on right. Straight, not right, then next turn right into High Street. Keep down High Street and go straight onto path where street bends to right near Post Office Stores. Immediately pass old stone wellhead on right and then quaint little conical market cross and war memorial.

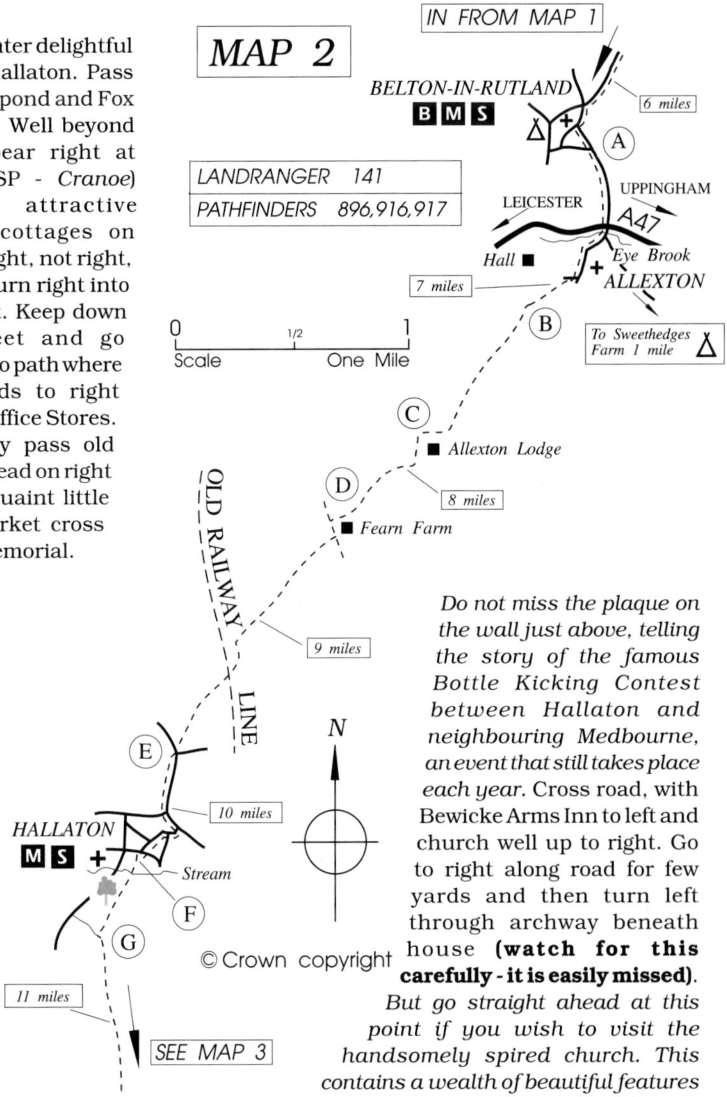

MAP 2

IN FROM MAP 1

BELTON-IN-RUTLAND
B **M** **S**

6 miles

LEICESTER   UPPINGHAM

LANDRANGER   141
PATHFINDERS   896,916,917

Hall ■

Eye Brook
ALLEXTON

A47

(A)

0   1/2   1
Scale   One Mile

(B)

To Sweethedges
Farm 1 mile

(C)

■ Allexton Lodge

(D)

8 miles

■ Fearn Farm

OLD RAILWAY LINE

9 miles

N

(E)

10 miles

HALLATON
M **S** +

Stream

(F)

(G)

© Crown copyright

11 miles

SEE MAP 3

Do not miss the plaque on the wall just above, telling the story of the famous Bottle Kicking Contest between Hallaton and neighbouring Medbourne, an event that still takes place each year. Cross road, with Bewicke Arms Inn to left and church well up to right. Go to right along road for few yards and then turn left through archway beneath house (**watch for this carefully - it is easily missed**). But go straight ahead at this point if you wish to visit the handsomely spired church. This contains a wealth of beautiful features including a stone flagged floor and some unusually attractive 19th-century stained glass windows. Also do not miss the impressive Norman tympanum in the porch depicting St Michael slaying a dragon.

(**F**) Now back on route - go down narrow path beyond archway *(having now left the Leicestershire Round County Path)*, over bridge crossing stream and over stile. Continue on same line up steep bank and across parkland passing end of wood on left. Good view back to Hallaton church and rectory.

(**G**) Through wooden gate at end of parkland and turn left onto track ignoring waymark sign on stile opposite. Go down track with hedges on both sides and attractive views ahead. Stubby spire of Slawston church visible over to right, with Slawston Hill to its left. At end of track, through wooden gate and head down left-hand side of two fields, with gate between them.

(A) Through third wooden gate and turn left onto minor road. After 100 yards, where road bends to left, turn right onto roughly surfaced byway going upwards.

(B) After three-quarters-of-a-mile go over x-rds (SP - *Weston*). *(But turn left if you wish to divert to Medbourne for a night stop - 1 mile.) Medbourne is a charming village, complete with several*

Springtime at Medbourne

pleasant 17th- and 18th-century houses, a stone built inn and a three-arched medieval packhorse bridge across a stream just below its substantial church.

(B) Back on main route - continue down pleasant road with high hedges on either side and good views ahead across broad Welland Valley. Just before going through gap in old railway embankment, cross course of Roman road which ran from Huntingdon to Leicester, but few signs of which remain.

(C) Soon pass bridleway signs on both sides of road. After almost half-a-mile go over small bridge crossing River Welland, which at this point is just to south of boundary between Leicestershire and Northamptonshire. For much of its length this river forms the boundary between these two counties. *Please note that throughout the course of its route through Northamptonshire the Macmillan Way will be waymarked by black and white signs provided by Northamptonshire County Council, rather than the normal green and white Macmillan waymarks.* Spire of Ashley church visible to south-east. Over hump in road by modern house on right, which probably replaced a level-crossing keeper's house, as we are crossing line of another old railway, signs of which are more apparent in cutting well over to right.

(D) Bear left at road junction (SP - *Ashley*) at entry to Weston-by-Welland with Wheel and Compass Inn on left. Soon bear right in centre of village onto B664 (SP - *Market Harborough*). *The village has a few pleasant ironstone houses and a church which was largely rebuilt in the 19th century.* Pass telephone box on right.

(E) Cross road with care just beyond first bend on B664 and through gate opposite stone house and into field. Go upwards, straight across field, through gate and straight across next field to reach small fenced gap near electric pole. Over fenced gap in hedge and head upwards, keeping to immediate right of hedge with minute wind turbine and at end of hedge turn left through large metal gate. Keep hedge on immediate right, then through gate. Turn right through second gate and follow hedge keeping to its immediate left.

(F) At end of hedge turn left near small building and small pond and follow track to left of hedge-line. Under high-voltage power-line, fine views to left of rolling Leicestershire country beyond Welland Valley. Through metal gate and keep hedge on immediate right. Through another metal gate and bear slightly to right following bending hedge-line. Good open, upland country here, as we pass small pond on right.

(G) Arrive at impressively tall, six-way concrete marker post. *We are joined here by the Midshires Way - a 225-mile long-distance path and bridleway linking the Trans-Pennine Trail near Stockport with the Ridgeway in Buckinghamshire. At times the 'Walkers Route' diverges from the 'Riders Route', but our route is common with the 'Walkers Route' as far as Maidwell - see page 6.)* Beyond six-way post keep in same direction with hedge-line on right aiming at spire of Brampton Ash church, which is about one-and-a-half miles to south-east. At end of field turn right through small gate and head down side of field with hedge to left. Good views across valley to Brampton Ash church, complemented by impressive line of mature ash trees in hedge to left of path. Through gate and continue on same line, but when ground starts to drop down ahead, turn left through small gate. Head almost due south down hill with hedge on immediate right, now aiming to right of Brampton Ash church.

(H) Now on edge of large field soon passing waymark post in valley and keeping to immediate left of hedge where it takes slight bend to right. Turn left at far corner of field and after about 40 yards, turn right through gate. Go slightly uphill, straight across small field to another gate. Turn left onto track after going through gate, keeping hedge on left *(watch for holes in path - badgers abound here !)* and follow around field by bearing right in next two half corners. Just beyond point where hedge comes in from left, turn left through gate and head diagonally across small field to cross stile to arrive at busy A427 by traffic layby.

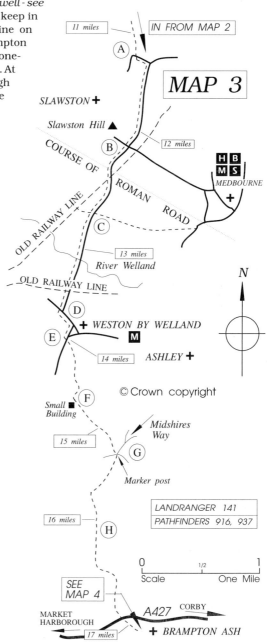

11 miles

IN FROM MAP 2

A

MAP 3

SLAWSTON ✚

Slawston Hill ▲

COURSE OF

12 miles

B

H B
M S

MEDBOURNE
✚

ROMAN ROAD

OLD RAILWAY LINE

C

13 miles

River Welland

OLD RAILWAY LINE

N

D

✚ WESTON BY WELLAND
M

E

14 miles   ASHLEY ✚

© Crown copyright

Small ■
Building

F

Midshires
Way

15 miles

G

Marker post

LANDRANGER 141
PATHFINDERS 916, 937

16 miles

H

0   1/2   1
Scale   One Mile

SEE
MAP 4

MARKET
HARBOROUGH

A427   CORBY

17 miles   ✚ BRAMPTON ASH

(A) Cross A427 with great care and over stile slightly to left. Now head diagonally left across field to immediate right of line of trees. Through wooden gate and head diagonally across next field aiming for right-hand end of tall Leylandii hedge. Good view of Brampton Ash church over to left. Through fence-line obliquely and pass end of Leylandii hedge. Through two wooden gates and turn right onto road *(But turn left and left again if you wish to visit church (usually locked). This is an impressive building with elegant broach spire, many lovely early-19th-century gravestones in its churchyard and two porches, both with tall doorways within.* Now back on main route and drop down into valley.

(B) Soon turn left off road through metal gate. Go to immediate right of attractive mellow-brick barns known as Red Hovel and through metal gate just beyond. Go quietly up field following to immediate left of hedge-line until reaching corner of Brampton Wood on left. Before turning right, look ahead, as deer from neighbouring woods often graze on the grass track visible from here.

(C) At this corner of wood turn right over small stone bridge to join the Jurassic Way. *The Jurassic Way is a Northamptonshire County Path, running for 88 miles between Stamford in Lincolnshire and Banbury in Oxfordshire. We not only follow it between here and Great Oxendon, but will also join it again between Eydon and Chipping Warden.* Through small gateway and over stile to go diagonally left across narrow belt of plantation and cross stile on its far side. Now aim for left-hand end of Hermitage Wood, beyond the brow. Join track running parallel with the left-hand (southern) edge of Hermitage Wood noting a mass of bluebells if you come here in May (Do not enter wood, which is private). Through several gates and eventually turn left onto road.

(D) Soon turn right on to busy A6 road (SP - *Market Harborough*) and after very short distance **cross A6 with very great care** and go through gap in hedge. Head

diagonally right aiming for mast on distant horizon (although this is not always visible) and once over first brow, head for gate. Through this metal gate and go straight downhill to stile immediately ahead. Through gate at end of hedge and drop down, going diagonally right and aiming for Park Hill Farm's buildings. Through metal gate to right of farmhouse and bear right to leave farmyard. Go straight across road and into field. Go diagonally left, aiming for white-painted stile. Over stile, under railway embankment and over second stile. Now turn right and go parallel with railway for short distance before bearing left to cross bridge over stream. Soon cross another bridge, turn left and follow to immediate right of hedge. Leave hedge where it turns left and head across field aiming to left of barns.

(E) Over double stile and turn right onto road. *Earthworks of Braybrooke Castle visible to right. Medieval home of the Latimer family and later, in Tudor times, of the Griffins, it must have once been an impressive building, but nothing now remains above ground.* Bear left

Bridge over the Jordan, Braybrooke

just beyond entry to Braybrooke and down School Lane (SP - *Arthingworth*). Keep straight along School Lane and turn right onto Griffin Road by Post Office Stores and Swan Inn (SP - *Market Harborough*). Pass village hall, cross River Jordan and then turn left into Newland Street by Baptist Chapel. B*ut turn right if you wish to visit the largely 13th-century church. This has a slender broach spire and a number of interesting monuments including one of Sir Thomas Latimer carved out of a single piece of oak. This local knight left money in his will for the completion of the three-arched bridge, which still spans the little River Jordan, just to the south-east of the church.* Back on main route - having turned left into Newland Street, follow road soon changing to dirt-surfaced track. Follow this, ignoring waymark to left, under high-voltage power-line and cross small bridge over River Jordan.

(**F**) Follow track as it bears sharply to left after stables on left. *(But bear slightly right off track, and onto footpath if you wish to link on to the Brampton Valley Way (see page 16) to go north into Market Harborough for overnight accommodation - two-and-a-half miles. It would be possible to walk south next morning, down Brampton Valley Way (see below) to re-join main route by tunnel entrance near Great Oxendon, a further two-and-a-half miles).* Back on main route - ascend small hill and look back for rewarding views north-eastwards across the Jordan valley to Braybrooke.

(**G**) About a quarter-of-a-mile beyond hill and about 50 yards before hedge converges from left, turn right off track onto path. Follow path across stile heading towards buildings on next hill *(Waterloo Lodge).* Down path into valley, crossing one stile, a pond on left and then another stile, before climbing directly up other side towards buildings. Cross stile, go up between fence on left and hedge on right and on brow of hill, cross yet another stile (passing to right of *Waterloo Lodge* - a series of converted farm buildings). Follow fence on immediate left, and cross stile just beyond metal gate in fence to left.

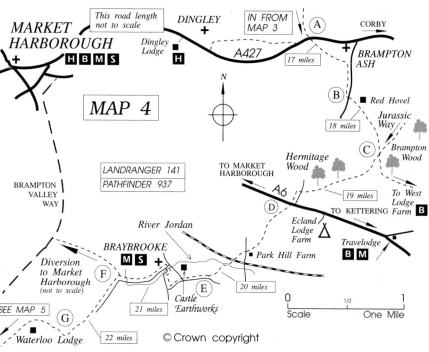

15

(A) Bear left to follow clear-cut path diagonally across grass and through spinney of young trees. Cross double-stile. Keep in same line across next field to go over treble-stile well to left of large ash tree. Keep in same line across next field, first aiming well to left of two large trees in facing hedge and once over slight brow, head for double-stile just to right of metal gate in far corner. Over this double-stile, go in same line, diagonally across next roller-coaster field, aiming for stile on edge of woodlands. Good view of Great Oxendon church over to right. In winter, ventilation shaft of railway tunnel just visible through hedge to left.

(B) Over stile, follow muddy path down through scrubby woodland and pass over twin tunnels of disused railway line (not usually visible from this

Entrance to Great Oxendon Tunnel

path). At far edge of woodland, branch right to go along bank and then down to disused railway line. *(Now leaving the Jurassic Way.) (But branch left and go over fields if you wish to divert to Great Oxendon for overnight stop - about 250 yards).* Now back to main route, having followed path down to where it converges with bed of disused railway line. Turn sharp right just before brick bridge and go back along line. *This is the Brampton Valley Way, which we shall be following for 4 miles. This is a 14-mile linear park based on a former railway line between Market Harborough and Northampton, the embankments and cuttings of which are rich with wildflowers. Some walkers may find this stretch rather bland, but we feel that it provides a pleasant contrast with some of the harder cross-farmland sections.* Now head southwards, taking left fork which is more heavily used. Enter left-hand (east) railway tunnel, which is over 300 yards long and a fine example of Victorian civil

engineering. The exit can always be seen as the tunnel is straight, but a torch would certainly be useful, especially for spotting possible puddles.

(C) Follow Brampton Valley Way southwards beyond tunnel. Pass old level-crossing which allows access on right to A508. Soon cross viaduct over small stream and about half-a-mile beyond, pass over small underbridge where footpath between Arthingworth and A508 crosses. Continue down Brampton Valley Way and cross infant River Ise, tributary of River Nene, which it joins at Wellingborough.

(D) Pass large depot, car park and picnic area on left before crossing minor road from Arthingworth. After some distance fork slightly left beyond picnic table to take higher of two tracks into left-hand (east) tunnel (see notes above on previous tunnel near Oxendon).

17th-century gateway at Maidwell

Beyond tunnel go under busy A14 road and again continue southwards on Brampton Valley Way. Cross line of bridleway between Harrington and Maidwell, pass Draughton Car Park and Picnic Area on left where we cross Maidwell to Draughton road.

(E) Soon turn right over stile leaving Brampton Way and Midshires Way near old metal footbridge (SP - *Maidwell Village*). Down across narrow field and over bridge with two stiles crossing brook. Head across field keeping to immediate left of hedge bending slightly round to left and aiming for Maidwell church. Through small gate at entry to Maidwell and join road by church on left and school on right. *The squat towered church is largely 13th and 14th century and contains a colourful 17th-century monument to Lady Gorges and her husband, Lord Dundalk.* Keep on road into centre of Maidwell passing elegant 17th-century gateway on right. This used to stand at the entrance to Maidwell Hall's kitchen garden and was moved a few yards to its present site in 1914.

(F) Cross busy A508 with great care (but turn right if you wish to visit Stag's Head (B&B) - just visible beside A508). Bear round slightly to left on surfaced road opposite to one from which we have just crossed (SP - *Dale Farm*) (ignoring footpath sign). Go along surfaced road past metal barns on left with fine views ahead as road drops down. Pass sign on left indicating 'Dale Farm Conservation Area' - pleasant piece of woodland. Bear left keeping on surfaced road as it bends round to left near entry to Dale Farm, ignoring both bridleway and footpath signs. Good views ahead as country opens out.

(G) Pass Blueberry Lodge barns and farmhouse on right, with track soon becoming less well surfaced and more interesting, first bordered by hedges and then with large open grass fields to left.

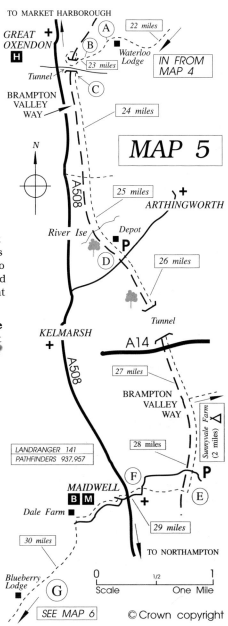

TO MARKET HARBOROUGH

GREAT OXENDON

Waterloo Lodge

IN FROM MAP 4

Tunnel

22 miles

23 miles

BRAMPTON VALLEY WAY

24 miles

MAP 5

25 miles

ARTHINGWORTH

River Ise

Depot

26 miles

Tunnel

KELMARSH

A14

27 miles

BRAMPTON VALLEY WAY

Sunnyvale Farm (2 miles)

LANDRANGER 141
PATHFINDERS 937,957

28 miles

MAIDWELL

Dale Farm

29 miles

30 miles

TO NORTHAMPTON

Blueberry Lodge

SEE MAP 6

0   1/2   1
Scale   One Mile

© Crown copyright

17

(A) Track becomes better surfaced again when ruined buildings of Blueberry Grange come into sight. Pass wood on right and derelict Blueberry Grange buildings on left. Through gateway onto surfaced road with parkland on right. Trees on right obscure views of park, but eventually there is a good but distant view of south-east front of elegant, early 18th-century Cottesbrooke Hall up avenue of young trees over to right. This may possibly have been Jane Austen's inspiration for *Mansfield Park*.

(B) Over road beyond large farm buildings on left, going slightly to left, through large wooden gate. *But turn right and walk along road if you wish to visit delightful Cottesbrooke village - the unspoilt Georgian interior of the church and elegant entrance gates to Cottesbrooke Hall making this well worthwhile.* Back on main route - having gone through large wooden gate, head for far right-hand corner of field. Over small stile to right of double gates, then go diagonally right, across field to large double gates and towards right-hand end of Creaton village which is visible on skyline ahead. Over small stile to right of double gates, over bridge crossing stream and immediately turn left and through more double gates. Follow along to immediate right of hedge with stream just to its left. Through wide gap at next hedge-line across path and bend slightly round to left near end of field.

(C) Through gap in hedge and turn right, going up hill to immediate left of hedge-line. Follow this line as far as road near entry to Creaton. Bear left onto road and enter pretty ironstone and brick village of Creaton. Bear right at first road junction (SP - *Welford*) and soon bear left at second road junction to climb up High Street. Bear left onto wider road beyond Post Office Stores on right, with church on left. Attractive village green well over to right. Leave Creaton by road up past church. Turn right with care onto busy A50 (SP - *Leicester*) and almost immediately cross road to go through metal gate. Follow well surfaced track down hill, going over stile by wooden gate and through area with wooden stables on right. Through gate beyond stable yard and another gate. Over double-stile and go diagonally half-right to cross footbridge.

(D) Bear right to cross small field to stile in right-hand corner. Cross stile, continue

up field keeping to immediate left of hedge, climbing out of valley and through gap in hedge at end of field. Keep up hill along same line as previously. Pleasant view of Hollowell village and church over to right. Now go to immediate left of re-started hedge. At end of this long field go over stile, down hill and veer right following to immediate left of curving hedge-line before starting to climb again. Pastures Farm visible over to right. Continue up hill, through large gap in fragmentary hedge-line coming in from left. Over stile in hedge and bear round to right following to left of hedge, soon passing small clump of trees on right before turning left onto road.

(E) Walk down road and bear half-left at five-way x-rds at entry to Teeton (SP - *Spratton*) (but bear left if you wish to visit Teeton, although no items of real interest here, apart from telephone box). **Walk with care, road verges are very narrow and traffic can be fast.**

Our path near Creaton

18

(F) Turn right at x-rds on bend (SP - *Holdenby*) and keep on road dropping gently down into valley, past old mill house on right and start to climb other side. At entrance to Holdenby North Lodge, by house on right, cross road and over stile by gate, leaving road to head across field diagonally half right. Soon aim for large metal gate in second fence (not immediately visible). Over stile by water trough and veer slightly left to pass between two clumps of trees. Over stile at far end of field and continue in same direction to aim for left-hand end of Holdenby woodlands. Over stile and aim for stone house (once a lodge).

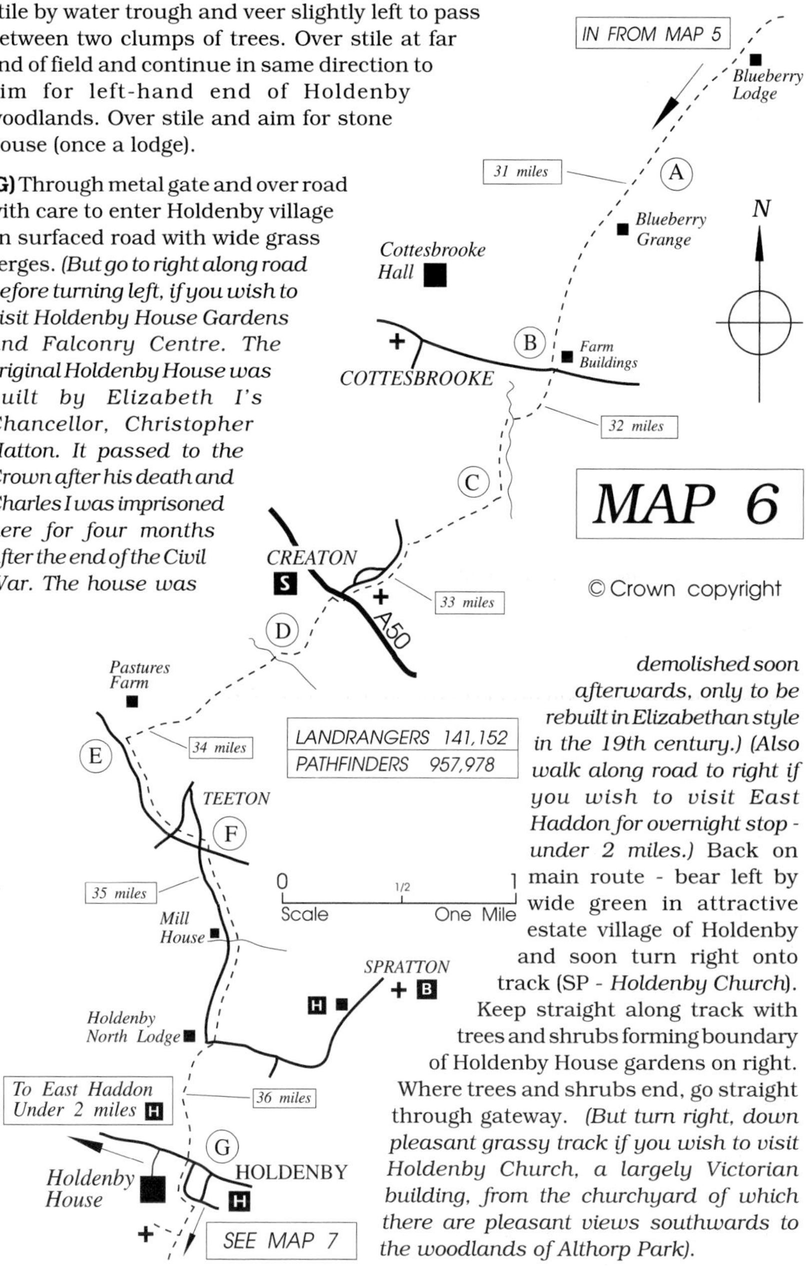

(G) Through metal gate and over road with care to enter Holdenby village on surfaced road with wide grass verges. *(But go to right along road before turning left, if you wish to visit Holdenby House Gardens and Falconry Centre. The original Holdenby House was built by Elizabeth I's Chancellor, Christopher Hatton. It passed to the Crown after his death and Charles I was imprisoned here for four months after the end of the Civil War. The house was* demolished soon afterwards, only to be rebuilt in Elizabethan style in the 19th century.) *(Also walk along road to right if you wish to visit East Haddon for overnight stop - under 2 miles.)* Back on main route - bear left by wide green in attractive estate village of Holdenby and soon turn right onto track (SP - *Holdenby Church*). Keep straight along track with trees and shrubs forming boundary of Holdenby House gardens on right. Where trees and shrubs end, go straight through gateway. *(But turn right, down pleasant grassy track if you wish to visit Holdenby Church, a largely Victorian building, from the churchyard of which there are pleasant views southwards to the woodlands of Althorp Park).*

IN FROM MAP 5

Blueberry Lodge

31 miles

(A)

Blueberry Grange

N

Cottesbrooke Hall

(B)

Farm Buildings

COTTESBROOKE

32 miles

(C)

MAP 6

© Crown copyright

CREATON

S

A50

33 miles

(D)

Pastures Farm

34 miles

(E)

LANDRANGERS 141,152
PATHFINDERS 957,978

TEETON

(F)

35 miles

Mill House

0   1/2   1
Scale   One Mile

SPRATTON

H   +   B

Holdenby North Lodge

To East Haddon Under 2 miles   H

36 miles

(G)

Holdenby House

HOLDENBY

H

+

SEE MAP 7

19

(A) Back on main route - having gone through gateway beyond turn to Holdenby church, continue in same direction down track across field with mound to right. Through gateway at bottom of field and keep in same direction with hedge on immediate left. Then turn right, following cross-hedge now to left and aim across next field for line of trees. Arrive at line of trees and through fence to follow to left of hedge-line with trees (If path to left of hedge is obstructed use track to right of hedge). Good views back to Holdenby House, above the church. Through gap in hedge at end of field and head straight across field on rough track aiming just to right of modern barns. Great Brington church visible on skyline ahead left, with woodlands to its left being part of Althorp Park. Still heading to right of barns.

(B) Through small gate and turn left near barns onto busy A428 and **immediately cross with great care to utilise wide verge on far side**. Beyond cottages on right go onto path beneath railway bridge and then turn right onto minor road (SP - *Great Brington*). (Regrettably we shall follow this road into Great Brington, but there is no alternative.) As our road bends slightly to right it is joined by the impressive stone wall of Althorp Park and we follow this for some distance up hill. *The splendid 17th- and 18th-century mansion of Althorp is hidden in its great park, well to our left. Althorp, the home of Earl Spencer, is open to the public at certain times.*

(C) Straight, not left near Great Brington entry sign, and then straight not right, with church up to left. *This is a fine building with a lovely old roof to its nave and many other interesting features. Its North Chapel has a splendid series of Spencer tombs, and although enclosed by spiked iron railings, these monuments are well worth looking at. The adjoining rectory, with its polygonal tower, has a rather Tudor flavour, but is in fact, an early 19th-century building. The village beyond is a pleasant mixture of stone, brick and some thatch, with many estate-built houses and cottages.* Beyond church, keep straight down village street, with war memorial on left and small triangular green on right, complete with large horse-chestnut tree and telephone box just behind it. Pass on right, Post Office and pleasant Fox and Hounds Inn (also called 'The Althorp Coaching Inn'). Bear round to right just beyond and leave village on footpath beside minor road.

(D) At about a quarter-of-a-mile beyond village, where road starts to bend to left, turn right at second of two footpaths, over stile and go diagonally across field following sign's direction. Over double-stile and ditch and go diagonally right across field following well defined path. Over stile at top of field and change direction slightly left, initially aiming for Little Brington church spire and then aiming for white disc marker just to right of small tin-roofed shed. Over combined fence, sleeper bridge and stile and up narrow field keeping to right-hand edge. Over stile and turn right onto road in Little Brington. (But turn left if you wish to visit village shop.) *This village has stone buildings, some of which are Althorp estate houses. Its Victorian church was demolished some years ago and all that remains is a handsome tower with broach spire - a rather sad landmark well away from the village.* Pass The Old Saracen's Head Inn on right keeping on road.

(E) Turn left at small X-rds roads before end of village and leave it on road passing last house on left *(Stoneacre)*, with stables just beyond. Soon turn left onto busier road, *which follows the course of a Roman road which ran from a settlement at Duston near Northampton to link with the Watling Street near Whilton.* After about 100 yards turn right at end of large layby down well-defined track with tall hedge on its left. Now descending into broad Nene valley with good views of hill country beyond. Keep on track through gaps in two successive cross-hedges with hedge still to our left. Targets of rifle range just visible below wood to left. Now turn left, through wooden gate at end of track and immediately turn right to follow hedge to immediate right.

(F) Ignore metal gate in hedge ahead and turn right before corner of field to cross stile and sleeper bridge. Cross field heading towards barns ahead and over stile and sleeper bridge in second corner. Bear left beyond stile and follow hedge-line to immediate left. Through low metal gate and turn right aiming for buildings of Vicarage Farm, but almost immediately, turn left over sleeper bridge and stile. Through narrow, young plantation and over second stile. Head straight across field keeping in same direction as previously, aiming to immediate right of line of trees along cross-hedge ahead.

(G) Over stile, pass between two narrow pools with signs of wildfowl and over second stile. Keep straight across field in same direction as previously, aiming for double gates, but go over two closely spaced stiles in hedge about 10 yards to right of gates. Go diagonally across field veering slightly to right of previous direction and aiming for gap in hedge with gate just to right of electric pylon. Through gate just to right of re-entrant corner of field. Now head diagonally across small field with pronounced dip. Over small stile half-way along opposite fence and go diagonally across

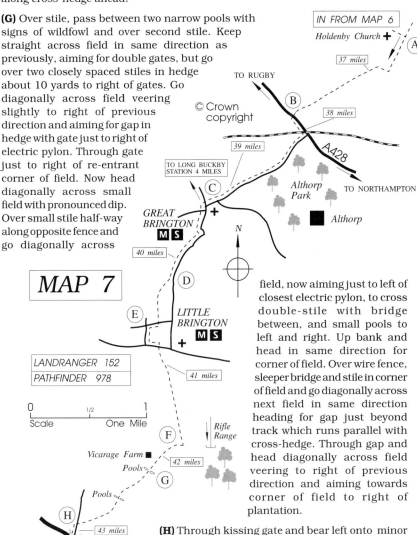

IN FROM MAP 6

Holdenby Church ✚

Ⓐ

37 miles

TO RUGBY

Ⓑ

38 miles

© Crown copyright

39 miles

A428

TO LONG BUCKBY STATION 4 MILES

Ⓒ

Althorp Park

TO NORTHAMPTON

GREAT BRINGTON **M** **S**

✚

■ Althorp

N

40 miles

MAP 7

Ⓓ

Ⓔ

LITTLE BRINGTON **M** **S**

✚

LANDRANGER 152

PATHFINDER 978

0 · · · · 1/2 · · · · 1
Scale · · · · One Mile

41 miles

Rifle Range

Ⓕ

Vicarage Farm ■

42 miles

Pools

Ⓖ

Pools

Ⓗ

43 miles

M1

A45

FLORE
H **M** **S**
✚ · SEE MAP 8

field, now aiming just to left of closest electric pylon, to cross double-stile with bridge between, and small pools to left and right. Up bank and head in same direction for corner of field. Over wire fence, sleeper bridge and stile in corner of field and go diagonally across next field in same direction heading for gap just beyond track which runs parallel with cross-hedge. Through gap and head diagonally across field veering to right of previous direction and aiming towards corner of field to right of plantation.

(H) Through kissing gate and bear left onto minor road. Immediately cross bridge over M1 motorway and after about 100 yards turn right over stile by gate. Immediately bear half-left and soon cross stile in fence. Now head across field aiming to left of white-painted garage at entry to Flore.

21

Chapter 2   Flore - Warmington   22 Miles

(A) Over stile by garage forecourt at entry to Flore and **cross often busy A45 with very great care (if busy, use controlled pedestrian crossing along to right)**. Go down Sutton Street, just to right of White Hart Inn. *Flore is a stone and thatch village, pleasantly quiet once away from the A45.* Telephone box soon on left. On edge of village, turn right at end of Sutton Street onto slightly busier road. Soon turn right at end of Nether Lane, into Spring Lane and almost immediately turn left to pass Brodie Lodge Playing Field notice. *Our path is now common with the Nene Way, a Northamptonshire County Path, stretching 70 miles between Wansford-in-England in Cambridgeshire and Badby, near Daventry. We shall share paths until reaching bridge over Grand Union Canal at Weedon Bec.* Up path with high hedges on either side, turn left by primary school, down road called *The Avenue* and into churchyard. *Looking out over the Nene valley from its tree-lined churchyard, the largely 13th- and 14th-century church has a stout tower and an interior with fine arcading and a medieval screen.* Go straight down churchyard, keeping well to left of church. Through kissing gate and go diagonally across large field following well defined path (much used by dog-walkers - tread carefully!).

(B) Over steel bridge crossing River Nene and follow well defined path bearing slightly to left. Over smaller bridge crossing minute stream and turn right keeping ditch and hedge on immediate right, aiming for right of garage (probably still white painted) at Weedon Bec. **Cross the still busy A5 with great care**. *(But turn left and walk with care up left-hand side of A5 if you wish to visit Narrowboat Inn - pub, motel and restaurant - but safer to go a little further along main route and then walk back along canal towpath.) The A5 follows the course of Watling Street - the road built by the Romans to link their channel ports to London and the great legionary fortress at Chester. It is interesting to note that this busy transport corridor, first opened up by the Romans, now carries not only the A5, but also the Grand Union Canal, the busy railway line beside it and the M1 motorway not far away.* Having drawn breath on far side of A5, take minor road (SP - *Lower Weedon*) and almost immediately bear left onto well surfaced track. Soon go straight, not left (left-hand track is to sewage works only) and start to gently climb up from Nene valley. Over bridge crossing Grand Union Canal. *A link here between the Macmillan Way and the Grand Union Canal Walk - a 140-mile long-distance path between London and Birmingham. The canal itself runs from Birmingham to the tidal River Thames at Brentford and has its origins in the closing years of the 18th century. The Nene Way turns right here and also uses the canal towpath for a short distance. (Use towpath to walk left to Narrowboat Inn more safely than along A5 (see above), or to walk right to Weedon with its several hotels, pubs and restaurants).*

(C) Go over busy railway line which runs parallel with canal here. Over stile beside metal gate and continue on track up hill. Church Stowe church tower soon visible

well over to left beyond valley. Turn sharp left off track immediately in front of metal gate and follow down edge of field with hedge on immediate right. At bottom of field go over concrete bridge and turn half-right to go up hill through very large field in general direction of Stowe church tower. *Loose oolitic (Cotswold) stone much in evidence in this field.* Over stile and continue in same direction up small, steeper field. Note

Well cleared path beyond Flore Church

22

fine views back over the Nene valley. Over another stile and cross bushy field with church up to left, and through small gate at entry to Church Stowe.

(D) Turn right onto road (but turn left if you wish to visit church). *Church and village are poised on a steep slope looking northwards over the busy and already remote Nene Valley. The church has a slender, largely Saxon tower and a small Norman north doorway. Within will be found two exceptionally fine monuments, a 13th-century armoured knight in Purbeck marble, Sir Gerard de L'Isle, and a beautifully carved Lady Elizabeth Carey, by the well-known 17th-century sculptor, Nicholas Stone. There is also a good wall monument to Doctor Thomas Turner, President of Corpus Christi College, Oxford, who died in 1714.* Continue on road through Church Stowe village, with minute Post Office on left and telephone box on right. Keep straight out of village on road, soon ignoring footpath sign to left and pass bench on left. Ignore second footpath sign to left, and eventually pass entry to *The Larches* bungalow on right.

(E) Soon bear right by small triangular green onto slightly busier road (SP - *Farthingstone*). Pass Stowe Heights Farm on right, entry to *Stowe Lodge* on left and Lodge Plantation on left just beyond. Beyond house on right, views start to open up ahead as road begins to drop slightly. Entry to wood known as Ramsden Corner Plantation on right. Almost immediately after this gateway, go through gap in hedge on opposite (left) side of road and immediately turn right to climb fence. Head diagonally across field following direction of fingerpost and soon aiming for stile in cross-hedge. Over stile and continue in same direction across narrow field to stile in hedge. Over stile and veer slightly left to follow defined path across field.

(F) Bear left to follow remains of wall-line for about 100 yards and then veer right aiming for left-hand end of narrow conifer plantation in valley. Drop down across this large field and over bridge to immediate left of conifer plantation. Continue in same direction aiming for slight gap in hedge below right-hand end of modern barn visible beyond opposite side of road. Through gap in hedge by way-mark post, bear left onto road and up hill soon passing Farthingstone entry sign.

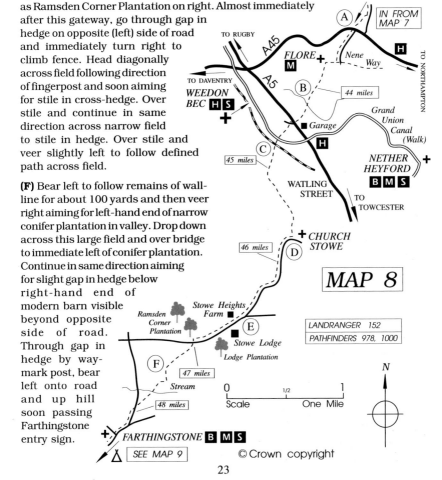

© Crown copyright

23

(A) Bear right at entry to Farthingstone keeping on road (SP - Everdon) and pass Post Office Stores and telephone box on left. Turn left by Kings Arms Inn on right and church ahead (SP - *Maidford*). *In Farthingstone, with its ironstone houses, cottages and neo-Tudor inn, we cross the Knightley Way, a 12-mile Northamptonshire County Path, between Badby, near Daventry and Greens Norton, near Towcester. The attractive church, also of ironstone,*

Canons Ashby House

has a 13th-century tower and sits comfortably in its churchyard across the road from the inn. Continue out of Farthingstone village, past entrances on left to *Littlecourt Yard* and *Little Court*, where road bends round to left.

(B) Soon, after telegraph pole on right, turn half-right through metal gate. Ignore obvious track along right-hand boundary of field and follow indistinct path diagonally left across field towards two ash trees in opposite corner. Go through large gap in hedge in corner of field into next field. Pass close to ash tree on right before turning half-left towards small gap in hedge ahead. Through gap in hedge, turn half-right to follow distinct path across field towards corner to left of three large oak trees. *Note radio beacon up to left - a strange-building looking almost 'extra-terrestrial'.* At corner go straight ahead through gap in hedge and over metal gate. Now follow left-hand hedge to gate visible in corner of field. Through metal gate and go straight ahead following right-hand hedge. Through three more gates to reach a metal gate at road.

(C) Over stile beside gate, turn right onto road and after 75 yards turn left onto byway track. Continue along byway past Tunningham Farm to reach T-junction with minor road.

(D) Turn left onto this road and go slightly up hill. Go straight, not left at road junction (SP - *Preston Capes*).

(E) After 500 yards turn left where road comes in from right to go through small gate (SP - *Byway*). Go along track, known as Oxford Lane, with hedge to right and open field to left. Soon passing wood on right known as Ashby Gorse.

(F) After small wood also on left, cross concrete farm road to continue on grassy track with hedge and trees on right. Immediately after cross-hedge comes in from right, turn right to go over stile. Tower of Canons Ashby church now visible ahead. Go diagonally left across field aiming for hedge corner to right of clump of trees

Quiet lane beyond Moreton Pinkney

in middle distance and to right of church tower. A hedge and gate soon come into view. Through gate and continue in same direction across large field. Follow line that passes close to hedge-corner sighted earlier and from there to right of single large ash tree. Through metal gate well to right of ash tree. Now go diagonally across park-like field with several mature trees, aiming for church tower with Canons Ashby House just to its right.

(G) Over stile opposite Canons Ashby House. *Home of the Dryden family since the 16th century, Canons Ashby is now owned by the National Trust and well worth visiting. Having escaped the attentions of 19th-century improvers, it is full of atmosphere and looks out over recently restored formal gardens to extensive parklands beyond. The poet John Dryden often visited his uncle here.* **Beware of traffic** but follow busy B4525 towards church (SP - *Banbury*). Continue on B4525 passing Canons Ashby church on left and bending to the left. *The church, with its massive tower, is the surviving west end of a 200-ft long church built by Black Augustinian Canons who had a priory here and, like the house, should not be overlooked.* Soon bear left keeping on B4525 (SP - *Banbury*) and **walk down it with great care**.

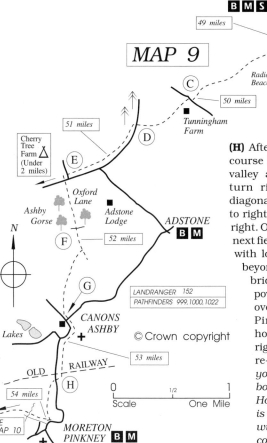

(H) After about 500 yards cross course line of old railway line in valley and almost immediately turn right to cross stile. Go diagonally left across field aiming to right of third power-pole from right. Over double-stile and cross next field aiming for gap in hedge with low gable-end visible well beyond. Over stiles and sleeper bridge, cross field passing power pole with waymark and over stile at entry to Moreton Pinkney. Down between house on left and wall on right. Go straight ahead to re-join B4525. *But turn left if you wish to use telephone box or visit the Olde House at Home Inn. Moreton Pinkney is an attractive stone village with two greens and many cottage gardens.*

25

(A) In Moreton Pinkney, soon turn right off B4525 into Brook Street just before reaching Victorian turreted archway. Go straight, not left, at small road junction and leave village by going over footbridge to right of ford. Immediately go straight, not left, and pass seat on right (this will confirm that you are on the right track and also provide an excuse for a rest). Now follow partly surfaced, hedge-lined track, bordered by trees in places. After half-a-mile go through metal gate, follow track on right-hand edge of field , and through second metal gate onto track with hedges again on both sides. Track soon bends to right with tall pine trees sheltering sad remains of long-vanished railway line running parallel on left - *this was the Great Central Railway - a line that never paid its way.*

(B) Soon turn left onto road to go over bridge crossing course of railway and almost immediately, where road bends to left, bear right up track which is a bridleway. Track soon starts to go downwards and becomes narrower path with hedge to left and fence to right. Through underbridge beneath embankment of another disused railway and bear left before going through thick cross-hedge. Keep on left-hand edge of field with broad grassy headland and then turn right at cross hedge to follow on right-hand edge of next field, also with grassy headland.

(C) Bear left at corner of field and follow right-hand edge with parallel stream bordered by rough grass and trees not far below to right. At bottom of field where hedge and trees come in from left, go to right, through gate, over bridge crossing stream and through second gate. Follow to right of line of trees bordering tributary stream and to left of electric power-line. Through gap in cross-hedge coming in from right and soon turn left onto surfaced track with hedge to left, climbing up to Eydon.

(D) Turn left onto road at entry to Eydon and immediately bear right up School Lane by entrance to Eydon Hall on left. *Here is a village green and stocks, and opposite it, on the corner, a lovely house with gabled, two-storeyed porch. Pronounced 'Eden' and not 'eye-don', this is a delightfully unspoilt stone village on a slight rise.* Straight, not right, at road junction (SP - Culworth) *(but turn left if you wish to visit the small, much restored church, with views of handsome 18th-century Eydon Hall from its churchyard, or turn right if you wish to visit the Royal Oak Inn.*

(E) Near end of village, where road bends to left, go straight ahead through small gate and then through large metal gate. Through small gate still keeping in same direction, with fence on left and hedge on right. Soon starting to descend into broad valley of infant River Cherwell. At bottom of bridleway are two stiles - go over left-hand stile, temporarily leaving bridleway and continue in same direction into small spinney with hedge on right. Over footbridge crossing River Cherwell. *This flows into the Thames at Oxford and is the first south-flowing river we have encountered.* Bear left and continue up left-hand edge of field with river and later, hedge to immediate left and at end of field bear round to right and go through second gap in hedge to left.

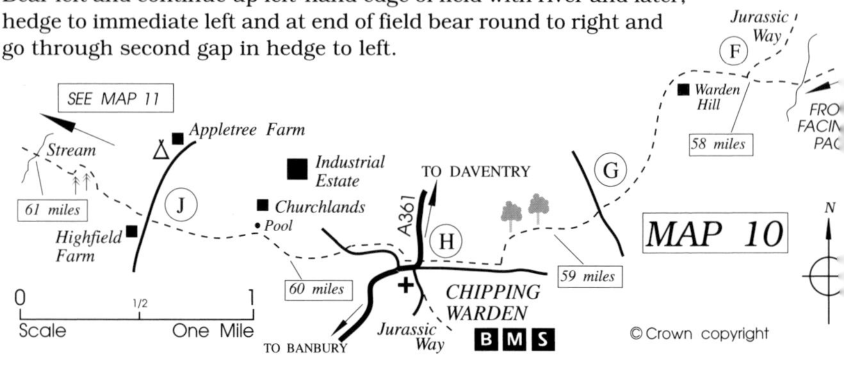

SEE MAP 11

Stream

Appletree Farm

61 miles

Highfield Farm

J

Industrial Estate

Churchlands
Pool

60 miles

TO DAVENTRY

A361

CHIPPING WARDEN

TO BANBURY

Jurassic Way

B M S

Jurassic Way

Warden Hill

58 miles

G

59 miles

FRO FACIN PAC

MAP 10

N

© Crown copyright

0   1/2   1
Scale   One Mile

F

(F) Through this gap, *where we are joined by the Jurassic Way (see page 14) coming in from left (we shall share paths with this as far as Chipping Warden).* Now up track to immediate right of hedge and turn sharp left onto new track where our track bends to right at top of slope beyond line of Leylandii. Along track with trees to left and view of large pool down to left. Bear left onto surfaced farm road and where road bends to left heading for Wardenhill Farm, go straight ahead through large double gates onto track with hedge on right and large conifers on left. Soon pass derelict farm cottages on right and at end of field go through small gate. Keep along top of field with fence to immediate left and slopes down to right. Bear slightly right away from fence line to aim for gate in hedge below.

(G) Through metal gate, across minor road and through gate. Head down left-hand edge of field aiming for waymark just beyond small brook. Cross brook and head diagonally right aiming for stile on edge of wood. Cross stile and along wide track through wood. *Many derelict air-raid shelters within spinney - there was a World War II airfield nearby.* Bear left at end of spinney and slightly left again onto surfaced road. Turn right, onto Culworth Road. Along road to enter Chipping Warden and pass Griffin Inn on right.

(H) Go straight ahead onto A361 by village green (SP - *Wardington*) *(but turn left if you wish to visit church or telephone box) (Now leaving Jurassic Way which goes to left here). Once a busy market town, 'Chipping' being the Old English word for market, Chipping Warden retains a flavour of times past. It has wide greens overlooked by thatched cottages and the remains of an old market cross near the impressive church.* Pass Rose and Crown Inn on right and turn right onto minor road (SP - *Appletree*). This road bends to left at end of village and then, where it bends slightly to right, go straight ahead, over stile and through area with caravans. Go to left of enclosure, over stile and along left-hand edge of field. Over stile into spinney and join track bearing diagonally left. Through gap and go diagonally slightly right along track. Continue in same direction to fence with no stile. Over fence and head diagonally left keeping to left of embanked pool near Churchlands (house), crossing possibly boggy ground. Through small gate at end of fence, turn right and shortly cross over three stiles plus possible electric fence. Continue straight ahead towards Highfield Farm keeping long hedge on immediate right. *Now entering Oxfordshire. Waymarks will be the standard 'Macmillan Green' from this point onwards.*

(J) Through metal gate, go across road by Highfield Farm and through large metal gates keeping to immediate right of low cowshed (now on permissive path). Go along field keeping as near as possible to left-hand hedge. Veer slightly right where hedge bends to right and soon go left through metal gate. Now keep to right-hand edge of field and soon bear right through gap to go down outside, right-hand edge of wood. Through metal gate at end of wood on left and turn sharp left, go about ten yards and turn right to head across field aiming just to right of oak

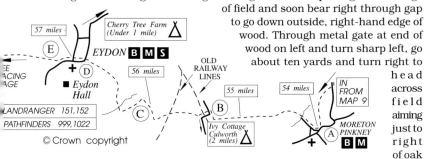

tree in hedge ahead (re-joining right-of-way). Claydon now visible ahead, well beyond valley.

(A) Go across small bridge to right of oak tree and head diagonally left across narrow field to probable waymark post in hedge to left. From waymark follow up field with small barn at end on right, keeping to immediate right of hedge. Through small gap in hedge in far left-hand corner of field. Through gap in hedge and through next field keeping hedge on immediate left. At end of field bear slightly right and then left through large gap into next field keeping hedge on immediate left. Turn left at bottom of field, bear left over footbridge crossing stream and go diagonally across field aiming just to right of canal bridge.

The Oxford Canal, near Claydon

(B) Over stile and bear left onto road by small parking area to cross bridge over Oxford Canal. *(But go through gate by parking area and turn right onto Oxford Canal towpath if you wish to explore up to Claydon Top Lock with its small shop.)* *The Oxford Canal, the work of James Brindley, was opened in 1790 to link the Coventry coal fields with the Thames at Oxford. Its towpath provides a fine walk over the watershed between the Midland Plain and the Thames Valley.* Now head westwards, straight up road and go straight, not left, at entry to Claydon (SP - *Claydon*). *Claydon is a quiet hilltop village less than two miles south of the point where the counties of Warwickshire, Northamptonshire and Oxfordshire meet. The little saddleback-towered church has Norman arcading with its supporting pillars no more than five feet high.* Bear round to right, pass Butlin Farm on right, with its very interesting Granary Museum of Bygones (don`t miss this) and immediately go straight, not left by church (SP - *Boddington*).

(C) Pass telephone box on right and turn left onto small road opposite house called *Latham*. Go down quiet road and **cross railway line with great care, noting warning signs stating 'Stop, Look, Listen. Beware of trains'.** Now entering Warwickshire. Go along farm track and pass large poultry farm on right.

(D) Now cross busy A423 with great care. Through gap in hedge next to signpost, almost opposite but slightly to left, and head straight across field. Through gap in hedge and bear slightly left aiming to left of houses near entry to Farnborough. Bear left at end of houses and follow round edge of playing-field, turning right at its far end before turning left onto road. Follow road through village passing Butchers Arms and telephone

MAP 11

To Avon Dassett 1 mile **B M**

FROM FACING PAGE

E

0 ——— 1/2 ——— 1
Scale One Mile

65 miles

TO WARWICK

SEE MAP 12

B4100

F

B4086 Village Green

WARMINGTON **B M**

M40

© Crown copyright

TO BANBURY

28

box on left, village shop on right and pathway up to church on left. *Farnborough is a charming Hornton-stone, hillside village with cottages and houses poised above its winding street. Although its spire is Victorian, the rest of the church is medieval and worth visiting. The National Trust's Farnborough Hall is a handsome, largely 18th-century house in modest parkland, the outstanding feature of which is its lovely terraced walk, complete with temple, pavilion and obelisk. Try to visit* this if open. Bear right at road junction near entrance to Farnborough Hall (SP - *Avon Dassett*) and soon bear left at next road junction down Dassett Road. *Good views of Farnborough Hall up to left and of lake to right, with wide grass verges either side. View of further lake down through trees to left and eventually there are views back to buildings and obelisk on Farnborough Terrace on hill slope to left.*

Farnborough Hall

(E) Turn left onto smaller, unfenced road (SP - *Warmington*) and go some distance before crossing bridge over ever-busy M40 motorway. Turn right off road immediately beyond top of motorway bridge, down steps and over stile. Head diagonally across field to its far left-hand side. Turn left in far corner of field, over footbridge and immediately turn right to cross 2nd footbridge. Now head diagonally left keeping well to left of sewage works. Over stile, cross roadway, over footbridge and continue in same direction across narrow field. Over stile and over yet another stile before turning right onto road at entry to Warmington. At this point we enter the Cotswolds 'Area of Outstanding Natural Beauty' and, apart from a brief exit to Shenington, we shall travel through it until reaching a point beyond Box in Wiltshire (see page 61, Point G).

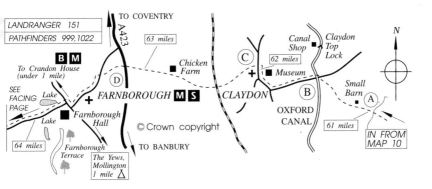

(F) Bear left and up road across village green. *This wide sloping green is complete with pond and sheep dip and is overlooked by a series of delightful Hornton stone houses and cottages, including an early-17th-century manor house and an elegant little Georgian rectory.* Pass Plough Inn on right and just beyond, leave road as it bears to right and go straight ahead up footpath steps, with churchyard on right. *The church stands in a churchyard shaded by pine trees and within will be found some very attractive rood loft stairs, Norman north and south arcading and a number of other interesting features.* Turn right onto footpath and go beside still busy B4100 at top of hill with church on right.

Chapter 3 Warmington - Maugersbury   24 Miles

(A) Leave Warmington church and go down hill on footpath beside still busy B4100. Soon cross entry to minor road coming in from right and just beyond first house on left of B4100, cross with great care and go up sloping driveway. Immediately turn right to go over stile and turn left to follow fence-line on immediate left. Pass house on left, through metal gate, between bushes and through second metal gate. Go between fences with farm buildings over to left. Through gate by water trough and keep in same direction along upper terrace with fence on immediate left. Splendid views out over the Avon valley including Farnborough Hall and the Burton Dassett Hills but sadly, much noise from the M40. Pass solitary beech tree poised above scarp face to right. At end of fence, over stile and turn left to head for metal gate below transformer on power-poles.

(B) Through gate, over B4086 and head slightly left to go through gate onto track with hedge on right. *(But turn right onto B4086 if you wish to visit Edgehill Country Park - about half-a-mile).* After about 100 yards turn right, over stile and down steep slope to stile in fence at bottom. Keep in same direction heading for gateway below oak tree on right. Keep in same direction across large field.

(C) Through large gateway crossing line of stream and bear left onto track between parallel hedge-lines. Bear round to right, keeping on track and where double hedge-lines finish, turn left through gateway, go steeply up field following line of power-poles, aiming just to left of power-pole on skyline. Through gate at top of hill and bear right, down terraced field to remains of stile to right of gate in valley bottom, keeping to right of line of power-poles. Over stile and head up hill aiming to left of farm buildings and over stile by power-pole. (B & B at farmhouse up to right.)

(D) Leave field and go left down surfaced farm drive into Ratley. Pass Rose and Crown Inn on left and bear slightly left by small triangular green. *A small, well sheltered village, Ratley has a grey stone church almost entirely in the Decorated style and a medieval cross in its churchyard.* Pass church on left, bear round to right keeping on road through village. *Earthwork up to left (on private ground) is known as 'The Mount' and was probably a gun emplacement built just before the nearby Battle of Edgehill (1642).* Leave Ratley going straight up road (SP - Edgehill).

(E) At T-junction cross road, into woodland joining the Centenary Way, which we shall follow for approximately two-and-a-half-miles. *Developed by Warwickshire*

County Council, this 98-mile recreational path runs from Kingsbury, south of Tamworth to Meon Hill, north of Chipping Campden. Down steep steps known as Jacob's Ladder and bear left keeping in woodlands, **not** going through gate into field. *Good views of Radway Grange in its parkland down to right. This was once the home of Sanderson Miller, 18th-century gentleman archi-*

The Vale of Red Horse from beyond Sunrising Hill   *tect and one of the pioneers*

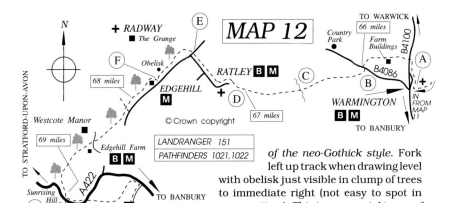

LANDRANGER 151
PATHFINDERS 1021, 1022

of the neo-Gothick style. Fork left up track when drawing level with obelisk just visible in clump of trees to immediate right (not easy to spot in summertime). *This is a memorial to one of Sanderson Miller's descendants.*

(F) At top of slope, turn right just before reaching Castle Inn in Edgehill village. *This was built as a folly tower by Sanderson Miller to mark the spot where the Royal Standard was raised at the outset of the Battle of Edgehill, on Sunday, October 23rd, 1642. There are fine views from the inn's terrace garden over the site of the battlefield and the Vale of Red Horse. Phone box just to north of inn.* Go down steep path behind Castle Inn, with railings to right. At bottom, bear left into woodlands and follow path along woods until joining track coming up from right. *This is known as King John's Lane, an old road that once came up from Kineton - where there is a mound known as King John's Castle. Sadly, there is no proven connection with that most maligned of all monarchs.* Immediately after junction with King John's Lane bear right, off it, onto narrow path between fence and upper edge of woods. Keep on clearly defined path for half-a-mile. Bear left up tarmac drive (which leads down to Westcote Manor - private) and almost immediately bear right keeping to immediate right of Edgehill Farm's building (B&B at farmhouse just up to left). Continue to follow path along upper edge of woods for another half-a-mile.

(G) Just beyond laurel bushes, **cross busy A422 with great care**. *Top of Sunrising Hill just to right. Layby car park with phonecard phone box 100 yards up to left. If you wish to visit National Trust's Upton House, walk up A422 beyond layby and immediately after this road bends to left, go across it to follow footpath over fields - half-a-mile. This handsome William and Mary mansion contains an outstanding collection of works of art and also has very pleasant, steep, sloping gardens.* Back on main route, after crossing A422 go down farm drive opposite, turn right down drive well before farm buildings, then left by post-and-rail fence and immediately fork left keeping on upper path. Through young plantation and metal gate into terrace-like open field with steep slopes to right and superb views over the Vale of Red Horse towards Bredon Hill and the distant Malverns. *The Vale of Red Horse takes its name from a hill figure which was once cut into hill slopes somewhere just south of here.* Keep across this field with fence to immediate left, and at its end, go through gate onto narrow path between hedge on left and wood on right.

(H) At junction of paths go straight ahead with fence on left and wood on right (*do **not** fork right down hill; the Centenary Way does, but we leave it here*). Now on special permissive path - not a right-of-way. Keep along path, eventually dropping down to farm drive in wood and turning left up drive, thereby re-joining right-of-way. Go up and along drive to arrive at road (Sugarswell Lane).

(A) Go straight across Sugarswell Lane, a sometimes busy minor road, and onto farm track. Keep down track between fences, almost immediately re-entering Oxfordshire. At end of track go through metal gate into field and keep along its crooked right-hand edge. *Pleasant views of valley down to right - this drains southwards as we have again crossed the watershed between the Severn and the Thames tributaries.* Over stile beside metal gate and keep down right-hand edge of field. Through hunting gate and keep straight in same direction down across field in now wide valley aiming for right-hand edge of wood coming down from left.

(B) Over concrete platform spanning dry hollow and veer half-right aiming to right of single oak tree and through wooden gate. Now keep to right-hand edge of field with stream immediately below to right. At end of field go through gap to immediate left of small building, but if ground impossibly boggy, use gate a few yards up to left. Then bear right to go through large wooden gate just below right-hand edge of coniferous wood. Along short track to right of wood, through second gate and keep in same direction across field. Shenington church tower soon visible over to right. Through metal gate, head for horse-jumps in middle of field and keep in same direction beyond them, aiming for gate in hedge ahead.

(C) Go through gate. *We are joined here by the d'Arcy Dalton Way, which comes in from left. This 65-mile recreational route runs southwards from the Oxford Canal near Wormleighton to link with the Ridgeway Long Distance Path near Wayland's Smithy. We shall follow it for about three miles, until reaching Epwell.* Keep straight, parallel with upper, wooded edge of field, along slight terrace, which becomes more track-like at its latter end at it heads slightly downwards. Through metal gate and head down across field veering slightly right to head for stile to right of low stone wall. Alkerton Church (see below) visible up to left. Over stile and through small boggy spinney (known locally as 'the osier beds') to go over two stiles with sleeper bridge between, crossing the Sor Brook. Go up field keeping to right of group of poplar trees and to immediate left of small, fenced orchard.

(D) Over stile at entry to Shenington and soon turn right onto road. *Standing over 500 feet above sea level, Shenington is a large, stone and thatch village grouped around a wide green. Its church was heavily restored in the 19th century by J.L.Pearson, best known as architect of Truro Cathedral. Neighbouring Alkerton, across the valley, has a smaller church but this has a real flavour of medieval times. If time allows, why not visit this and also the attractive garden of nearby Brook Cottage.* Pass Shenington church and school on left and keep on widest road across village green, with Bell Inn over to right. Keep straight out of village on road and immediately after *Agdon* (last bungalow on left), bear left off road and over stile.

(E) Go down field keeping to immediate right of fence. Over bridge crossing stream and head up bank to top left-hand corner of field. Streams here flow south and east to the Cherwell, thence to the Thames. Over stile by gate at top of field. Keep to immediate right of fence line and through small gate at end of field. Drop down into valley, following slight signs of stony track, to cross bridge over stream. Note ancient terracing especially to left.

Hill country beyond Sugarswell Lane

32

Through gateway and head diagonally left along slight signs of track with pool well down to left. Over stile crossing fence and go slightly left heading for near left-hand end of next fence line to cross a small bridge. Go diagonally left for about 25 paces to small stile in hedge and go diagonally up across field and once over brow, drop into valley aiming for waymark in far right-hand corner of field. Over bridge across minute brook and head up hill diagonally right, aiming for highest power-pole. Go to far left corner of field aiming to left of farm buildings and over stile onto road.

(F) Turn left onto road by Yarn Hill Farm and almost immediately turn right through metal gate (SP - *Epwell*) and onto farm track first keeping to less muddy, left-hand side and then following hedge-line on right. This track is heading between Yarn Hill on left and Epwell Hill on right. **About 120 yards short of the next gate watch out for possible loose fitting drain cover in grass - it could be very dangerous.** Through large metal gate and keep to left of hedge-line for short distance before heading slightly to its left, in direction of radio mast on horizon. Epwell village now visible ahead. Over three stiles crossing wooden fences and following hedge-line to right (ignore waymarked stile in hedge to right) and after third stile head diagonally left across small field with brook on right, then cross brook to post on edge of garden. Cross this quietly and through gate into Epwell.

(G) Bear left on road by village green, over footbridge beside ford and up road to centre of Epwell. *This small Hornton-stone village with its modest little church and welcoming inn is tucked away in a hollow amongst small bumpy hills.* Pass telephone box on left and bear right by village hall on right. Bear left on road (sign - *Max Width 7'0"*) keeping churchyard on left (footpath to Chandler's Arms on left beyond churchyard) *(We leave the d'Arcy Dalton Way here).* Soon after our road bends to right, turn left beyond 30 MPH sign onto footpath between private gardens. Bear slightly right in field and head up to left of hedge-line on right. Over stile at end of field *(crossing the ill-defined course of a Roman road that ran from Alcester and Stratford towards Kings Sutton, south of Banbury)* and turn right and then left to follow right-hand edge of field aiming for radio mast on horizon. (Ignore way-marks on stile to right.) Through metal gate and keep in same direction.

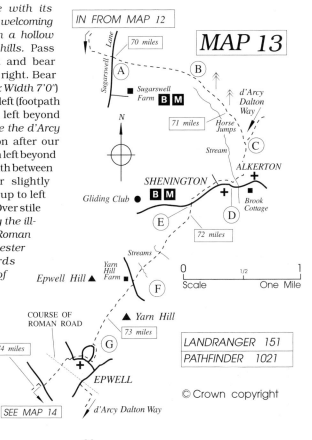

IN FROM MAP 12

MAP 13

70 miles

Sugarswell Lane

A

B

Sugarswell Farm B M

d'Arcy Dalton Way

N

71 miles

Horse Jumps

Stream

C

ALKERTON

SHENINGTON

Gliding Club ● B M

Brook Cottage

D

E

72 miles

Streams

Yarn Hill Farm

Epwell Hill ▲

F

COURSE OF ROMAN ROAD

▲ Yarn Hill

73 miles

74 miles

G

EPWELL

SEE MAP 14

d'Arcy Dalton Way

0   1/2   1
Scale   One Mile

LANDRANGER 151
PATHFINDER 1021

© Crown copyright

33

(A) Through large wooden gate, turn right onto road and very soon turn left through metal gate. Head straight across field aiming to right of radio mast and over stile about 50 yards to right of mast. Turn left onto Ditchedge Lane, *a green road that here forms the boundary between Oxfordshire and Warwickshire. This trackway may have been part of a prehistoric trade route, but it is more likely to have Anglo-Saxon origins. Although there is now no ditch alongside it, there may once have been one marking the boundary between the two counties.* We shall now follow Ditchedge Lane for some two-and-a-half miles and route-finding will be comparatively simple. Much of the lane is on a ridge and there are fine views both to right and left. Pass radio mast on left and into more sheltered length of lane, with pleasant glimpses to right of the spire of Winderton church, the impressive tower of Brailes church and Brailes Hill, topped with its clump of trees.

(B) Go straight ahead joining B4035 for short distance, before bearing left at next bend just beyond Warwickshire County sign, re-joining Ditchedge Lane. Keep straight along this green road with its fine views both to left and right. At end of third field on left, pass unsigned bridleway to left running between parallel hedges and leading to Sibford Gower - a possible diversion. *It would be possible to re-join main route further along Ditchedge Lane, or beyond Traitor's Ford.* Just beyond Round Hill to right, at end of hedge-bordered section of Ditchedge Lane, through gate into field following same line as lane and still following county boundary, with hedge to immediate left. Now start to drop down into upper valley of River Stour with fine views over to right including Broadway Tower, on the distant Cotswold skyline almost due west. At bottom of long field follow path along small sunken section of track and through gate onto minor road.

(C) Bear left and over bridge beside attractive ford with woodland on both sides of road. *This is known as Traitor's Ford, but the origins of its name are shrouded in mystery - some think that a traitor was killed here, others believe that its was once known as Traders' Ford, the traders using it during their journeys with pack animals along Ditchedge Lane.* Up wooded hill on minor road, soon going straight, not left, at first road junction (SP - *Whichford*) and then turning right at second road junction (SP - *Whichford*). Keep on minor road for about half-a-mile.

(D) At first hedge-line on left beyond New Barn farm buildings turn left through gateway. Go up track keeping to immediate left of fence and hedge-line. Bear right through first gate and then through second gate. Go half right, follow slight signs of track down field and over stile beside gate at bottom of field. Down hill keeping to left of scanty hedge and tree line and at its end, bear half-left heading for bottom left-hand corner of field. Over stile and bridge, up small lane into quiet valley hamlet of Ascott and soon turn right onto path immediately beyond gates of first house on right. Up narrow path between hedge and fence and over small stile into old orchard. Over second stile and turn left onto minor cul-de-sac road.

(E) Turn right at x-rds by Coombe House and follow path beside minor road heading towards Whichford. Bear left at road junction by small triangular green and enter Whichford, *an unspoilt village below the steep scarp face of the Oxfordshire Cotswolds.* Keep straight, not left, at wide village green (SP - *Stourton*) and pass Norman Knight Inn on right.

Traitor's Ford

34

Bear left by War Memorial at end of green with telephone box on left. Pass elegant 18th-century Old Rectory on right and church just beyond on right. *Whichford church has a Norman south doorway, an early 14th-century tower and a beautiful Perpendicular clerestory.*

(F) Well beyond church turn left up Roman Row - a small housing estate. Remains of medieval moat visible over to right at this junction. Over stile on left at end of Roman Row. Continue in same direction with hedge on right and at end of hedge turn half-right to go diagonally up hill following imprecise track towards tall tree. Beyond tree, keep just outside left-hand edge of Whichford Wood for about a mile, passing through gaps in two hedge-lines. Go over x-rds of tracks and onto track just inside wood, soon dropping down into valley.

(G) After nearly a quarter-of-a-mile turn left just beyond valley bottom onto track leading down valley. Through gateway at end of woods into field, keeping on track along right-hand edge of field with hedge and fence to immediate right. Long Compton church visible in valley ahead. Through metal gate beyond woods on right, still keeping on track, with hedge now to immediate left and open field up to right. Through gate at end of field and continue on harder surfaced track, which is now between two high hedges. Through metal gate and head straight across field passing large pond on left (Signed - *'Danger'*) and through metal gate to left of house. Onto surfaced driveway at entry to Long Compton and turn left with care onto A3400 (SP - *Woodstock*).

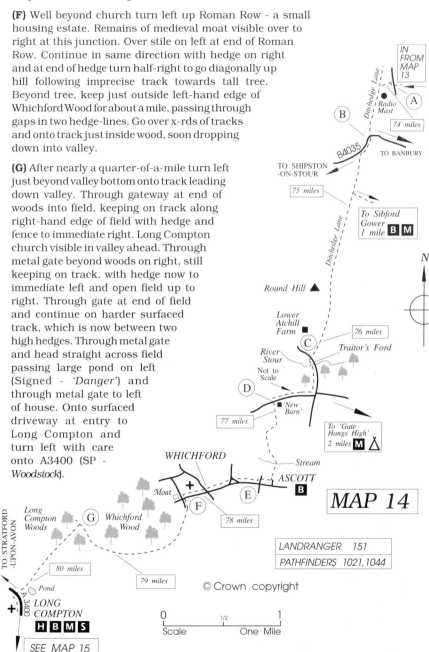

(A) Having turned left onto A3400, follow it through Long Compton, keeping to pathway on left. *Sitting beneath the high Cotswold edge, Long Compton has many attractive stone houses and cottages strung out along the still busy A3400.* Pass Crockwell Street on right *(go down here and soon onto path if you wish to use camp site at Mill Farm - three-quarters-of-a-mile).* Pass church on right *with its handsome Perpendicular tower and charming thatched lych-gate.* Manor House (B&B) on left, Post Office Stores on right. Base of old cross on stone plinth on right just beyond. Pass road to left signed B&B, which leads to telephone box and to Butler's Road Farm.

(B) Just beyond this road junction, turn right off A3400 beyond Village Hall on right, going through wooden gate with stone gate pier to left inscribed 'Daddy's Bank'. *(But go straight ahead for few yards if you wish to visit Red Lion Hotel and Restaurant.)* Through second wooden gate and head slightly left across field, first going on part of concrete track, to go through gate in wooden fence. Keep in same direction to go over stile beside metal gate, then go slightly left and bear right to follow well surfaced private road with hedge to right *(it may be possible to follow path to right of hedge - if so, this will be clearly marked)*. Leave surfaced track where it bends to right and continue in same direction on rougher track keeping hedge and ditch on immediate right and passing large converted barn beyond hedge on right. Where track bends to right, go straight ahead up field and then bear slightly left to head for far left-hand, top corner.

(C) Over stile at this corner and head straight up hill across field following well used path, keeping to immediate right of spring. South Hill Farm soon visible ahead. Through metal gate and first head towards centre of farm buildings, but soon converging with hedge line on right. Bear right over stile and follow line of hedge on right, with farm buildings to left. Where hedge finishes, keep in same direction across field, aiming well to right of radio mast with reflectors.

(D) Over stone stile and join road keeping in same direction and return briefly into Oxfordshire. *(But if you wish to visit the Bronze Age stone circle known as the Rollright Stones, turn left onto road, go straight, not left, turn left and go straight not left again - about one mile. This diversion is worthwhile and not as difficult to reach as the route directions would imply!)* Back on main route again - fine views westwards to Gloucestershire Cotswolds over to right. Just beyond point where road bends to right, go through metal gate on left (back into Warwickshire) and immediately bear right onto bridleway to follow along left-hand side of wall, thus continuing in same general direction. Oakham Farm soon visible down to right and good views ahead right, out over Evenlode Valley. Soon, near point where wall comes in from right, cross to right-hand side of our parallel wall, but continue in same direction. Follow farm track in same direction for about a mile with Little Compton visible down to right. Through small metal gate beside large one below

Dovecote opposite Chastleton House

power-pole with transformer, and note sign beyond on left regarding quarry workings. Keep in same direction with quarry to left and wall to right.

(E) Pass quarry and farm buildings on left, **cross busy A44 with great care** and onto minor road (SP - *Chastleton*) (But turn left if you wish to visit Cross Hands Inn - meals). Entrance to Grey Goose Farm (B&B) on left of main route just beyond A44. Through gate beside cattle-grid onto unfenced road, having just re-entered Oxfordshire and through pleasant parkland with grass and trees (Notice states - *Private Property - No Parking, Camping or Picnicking*). Pass two farmhouses down to right and at end of unfenced road through gate ignoring bridleway sign to left, and turn right onto minor road.

(F) Go down hill, passing attractive 18th-century arched dovecote in field to left, Chastleton Church and Chastleton House on right. *Chastleton House is, at the time of writing, being extensively restored by the National Trust, but it is hoped that it will be open to the public in 1997. This fine Stuart manor house was probably designed by Robert Smythson, the architect best known for Hardwick Hall in Derbyshire. It has a handsome five-gabled south front and an interior largely undisturbed by 18th- or 19th-century alteration, the most impressive feature of which is its Long Gallery at the top of the house.* Almost immediately turn left through large wooden gate (not signed, as use of this next short section is kindly allowed for Macmillan Way walkers only, by the National Trust and the owner of nearby Harcombe, and is not a right-of-way. Up lovely avenue of trees and soon go through small metal gate passing from Oxfordshire into Gloucestershire and returning to right-of-way.

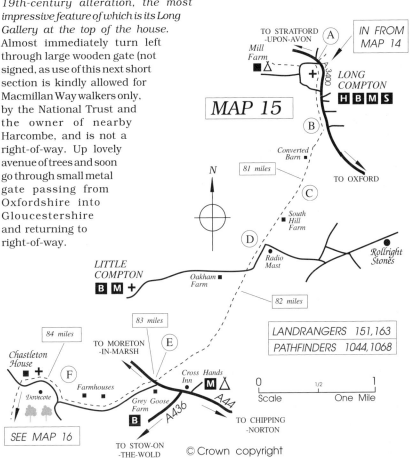

© Crown copyright

37

(A) Now head diagonally right, across field on well used track. Stow-on-the-Wold church just visible on skyline over to right. Over brow and start to drop down heading for waymark to left of two trees. Over stile by wooden gate beyond waymark and continue in same direction down field. Over stile following right-hand of two waymarks and continue down field keeping fairly close to right of hedge-line. Beyond large tree near end of field, bear left over stile, and immediately bear right, now keeping to left of remaining hedge-line and keeping in same direction. Soon over another stile with hedge converging from left. Initially follow line of hedge to immediate right, but where it bends to right, head diagonally left across field aiming for waymark on stile. Over this stile and onto track with hedge to left.

(B) Pass farm buildings on right and at entry to Adlestrop go over road junction onto minor road by bus shelter with the old Adlestrop Railway Station sign board. *This stands as a tribute to Edward Thomas, whose highly evocative poem* Adlestrop, *begins thus, 'Yes, I remember Adlestrop ...'. Sadly he died in France in 1917, aged only 39. The opening verse of his poem is recorded on a plaque on the seat.* Follow minor road into pretty Adlestrop village with its flower-filled cottage gardens and bear right by small Post Office (SP - Church). Bear right by church and then bear left down track between churchyard wall and Old Rectory; *this was often visited by Jane Austen, when her uncle, Theophilus Leigh, lived here.* Through small gate keeping on track between fences, with small lakes visible ahead and over to right. Views back to Adlestrop Park, the south-west front of which was designed by Sanderson Miller of Radway (see page 30). Through small gate beside large one and head diagonally right, and to immediate left of cricket pitch's low boundary fence. Skirt round about a third of cricket pitch's perimeter and then aim to left of long lake. After short distance head for footpath fingerpost now visible ahead.

(C) Over two stiles and turn left onto minor road. Almost immediately turn right with care onto A436 and keep on path along its right-hand side. *Over bridge crossing Isambard K. Brunel's London to Worcester railway line, with view to right of remains of station immortalised by Edward Thomas (see above).* Then over infant River Evenlode and soon cross to path on left-hand side of road. Turn left onto minor road (SP - *Lower Oddington*) and soon enter attractive village of Lower Oddington. Follow round long bend to right by Fox Inn and turn left at road junction by Post Office (SP - *St Nicholas Church*).

(D) At bottom of hill, turn right just before drive to New Rectory Farm on right, and through gateway where road bends to left in valley. *But go straight ahead for 250 yards if you wish to visit fascinating St Nicholas's Church. This is an ambitious, largely 13th- and 14th-century building with a remarkably unspoilt interior. See especially the lovely old chancel roof and the extensive 'Doom' wall paintings.* Back on main route - go straight across middle of narrow field, through kissing-gate and continue in same direction keeping to immediate right of hedge. Through another kissing-gate, cross small brook and up narrow pathway between two walls with house on right. Join road at eastern end of Upper Oddington and continue in

Memories of Edward Thomas at Adlestrop

same direction passing drive on left to Banks Farm (B&B). Bear left at road junction just beyond and up road for about a quarter-of-a-mile, with Horse and Groom Inn on right and telephone box on left.

(E) Keep on road out of Upper Oddington and turn right over stile just beyond last house on right. Down grass walk between two fences, over stile and head diagonally left aiming for yellow waymark just below power-pole in hedge across field. Do not go over waymarked stile but turn left to follow up to left of hedge. Where hedge turns to right, continue up across field aiming just to left of grass-covered reservoir. *Good views back from here include distant Brailes Hill, with its clump of trees and, much closer, Warren Hastings' beloved Daylesford House, built by him after retiring from his controversial career as Governor of Bengal.* Turn right through kissing gate to left of reservoir and go between reservoir fence on right and hedge on left. Into field keeping to immediate right of hedge and follow this line behind rugby club's pavilion and along left-hand edge of club's grounds. At end of grounds turn left through wooden gate and go down grassy track.

(F) Turn right onto B4450 and walk carefully along here on right-hand side to face oncoming traffic - road is quite busy and verges are narrow. Soon pass Fairview Farmhouse (B&B) on right and good view of Stow-on-the-Wold church ahead. Turn left off B4450 immediately before reaching the A436 (SP - *Maugersbury Village only*). Follow road into Maugersbury, *a pleasant village with lovely views across valley to Icomb Hill.*

(G) Bear left in Maugersbury by small green and telephone box on right (SP - *Maugersbury only*). *(But turn right if you wish to visit Stow-on-the-Wold - half-a-mile. To re-join main route at Map 17, Point A, walk down path beside A429 Fosse Way.) The attractive little market town of Stow-on-the-Wold is the focal point of the northern Cotswolds. Its Market Square is lively with visitors and local country shoppers all year long and it has all the facilities required by users of our Way including an excellent Tourist Information Centre and a number of B&Bs, hotels, inns and eating places.* Main route bears round to right keeping Dower House on left. Pass Manor Farm on right and keep out of village on road despite twin *No Through Road* signs.

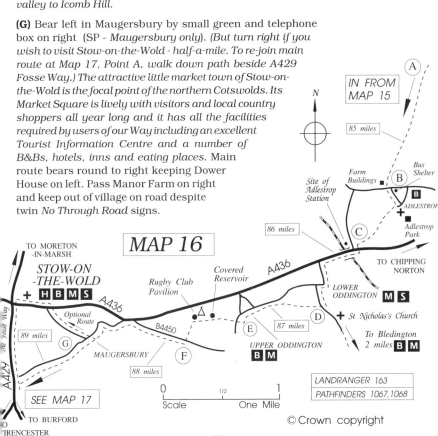

Chapter 4 Maugersbury (Stow-on-the-Wold) -
The Tunnel House Inn, Coates   26 miles

(A) About a mile beyond Maugersbury, through road barrier and turn left to follow wide path down beside the very busy A429 (SP - *Cirencester*). (If you have taken the diversion via Stow-on-the-Wold, re-join the main route here.) *The A429 follows the course of the Fosse Way. This was built by the Romans a few years after their invasion of Britain in 43AD and ran for 182 miles, between Lincoln and Exeter. For much of its course the Macmillan Way runs parallel with the Fosse Way and it crosses it twice - here below Stow, and later, near Castle Combe in Wiltshire.* At bottom of hill turn right and **cross A429 by traffic lights with great care**. Go down left-hand of two drives (SP's - *Private Drive to Hyde Mill* and *Bridleway to Lower Swell*). Follow well surfaced road past woodlands, cottage and farm to arrive at gate into Hyde Mill driveway. Go through gate and between avenue of poplars before bearing right by Hyde Mill House.

(B) Turn left over bridge (SP - *Lower Slaughter*) crossing mill pound *(this is formed by the Dikler, a stream which rises at Donnington Brewery lake and which, at Bourton-on-the-Water, flows into the River Eye, itself a tributary of the better known Windrush. We shall now share paths with The Heart of England Way as far as Lower Slaughter. This 120-mile long-distance path runs between Milford in Staffordshire and Bourton-on-the-Water, just to the south of Lower Slaughter.* (Follow Heart of England waymarks as far as Lower Slaughter.) Keep straight past houses, then bear left (SP - *Lower Slaughter*). Bear right at end of last house (SP - *Lower Slaughter*) and along track crossing flat valley. Over very small stream, turn left through gate and straight across field (very boggy here in winter), with little River Dikler on left. Over stile with Dikler just to left and head across field towards next gate with the Dikler veering away to left. Through gate and continue in same direction to cross fenced ditch before changing direction slightly to right. Cross another fenced ditch and almost immediately through gateway.

(C) Now head diagonally right aiming for waymark by gateway at end of field. Through gateway (SP - *Lower Slaughter*) and head for stile and gate at bottom right-hand corner of field. Through stile to right of gate and head diagonally across short field aiming for waymark. Over small bridge and stile and turn right to follow round edge of field before shortly turning left in corner, with wood now to right. Now aim straight towards Lower Slaughter Manor (now a hotel) along a broad grassy headland with hedge to immediate right. But just before end of field, turn right

through metal gate and then immediately left, with hedge now on left, thus maintaining previous line. Over stile and into sports field keeping to its left-hand edge.

(D) Through small wooden gate behind sports pavilion onto path at entry to Lower Slaughter. Now bear right onto driveway and then bear left onto road by corner of churchyard. Pass church on left and bear right at

Lower Slaughter

40

road junction by Washbourne Court Hotel (SP - *Upper Slaughter*). *Now briefly on the Wardens' Way - a 14-mile walking route between Bourton-on-the-Water and Winchcombe.* Walk up village on quieter, right-hand side of stream - the little River Eye, which flows into the River Windrush just below Bourton-on-the-Water. *Most of this delightful and much visited village seems almost to have been planted upon the banks of its stream. Stop here awhile if you are fortunate enough to arrive here at a quiet time.* Cross stream by small stone bridge (but go straight ahead if you wish to visit the interesting Old Mill Museum and Shop). Over 'main road' onto smaller road by Kingswell Cottage *(Now leaving the Wardens' Way).* Leave Lower Slaughter and climb out of valley, but do look back at mill with its water wheel and little brick chimney.

(E) Over x-rds with care, crossing minor road and onto track. Pass small wood in field to left as track levels out. Views of bustling Bourton-on-the-Water well over to left. Start gentle descent into Windrush Valley and cross road to go through small gate. *The road we have just crossed is known as Buckle Street. It acquired its name in Anglo-Saxon times, but its origins are probably much earlier.* Head diagonally right across large field aiming for far right-hand corner and go through small metal gate.

(F) Bear left onto well defined track with wall to left and soon through large metal gate. Keep on track with wall to immediate left (still dropping down into valley) and then through wooden gate and down track, now overhung with trees, with narrow field to right. Bear right at junction of bridleways, *joining the Windrush Way - a 14-mile walking route between Winchcombe and Bourton-on-the-Water.* Down wide, surfaced path curving left to surfaced road with houses on right. Over River Windrush and immediately start to climb out of valley. Bear slightly left by entrance roadway to Aston Farm on right, *now leaving the Windrush Way.* Few signs are now visible of railway line that once crossed road here. Almost immediately bear right keeping on surfaced road, ignoring waymark on left. Up steep little pitch and then turn right to walk up field to immediate right of hedge and wall, which soon bears left by tree. Pleasant views back over the Windrush Valley from here.

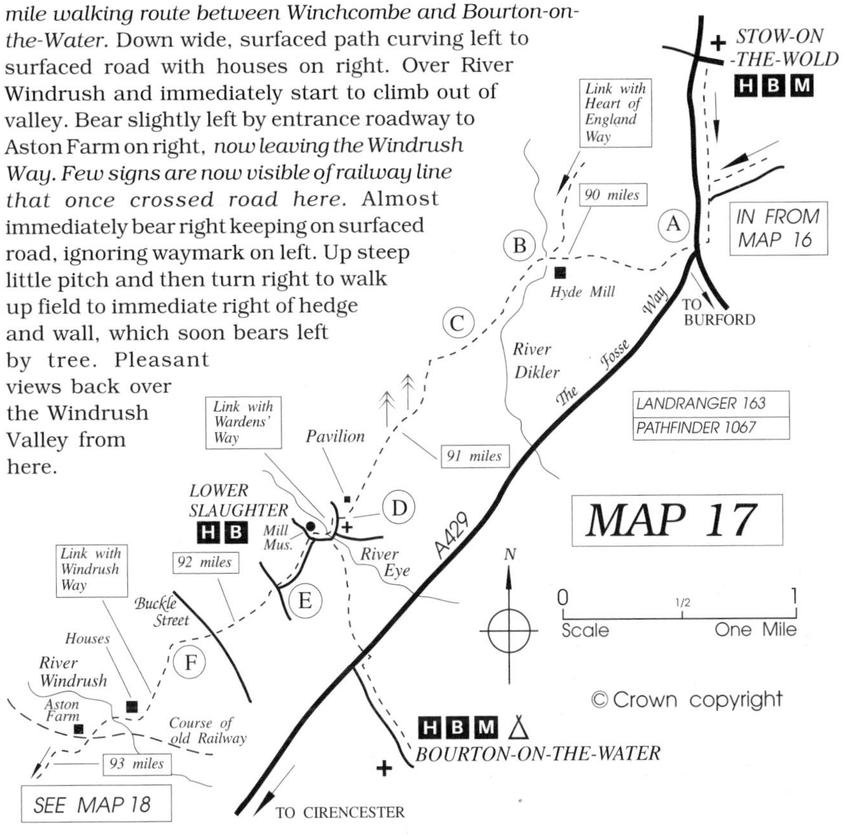

STOW-ON-THE-WOLD
H B M

IN FROM MAP 16

Link with Heart of England Way

90 miles

A

B

Hyde Mill

TO BURFORD

C

River Dikler

The Fosse Way

LANDRANGER 163
PATHFINDER 1067

Link with Wardens' Way

Pavilion

91 miles

MAP 17

LOWER SLAUGHTER
H B
Mill Mus.

D

River Eye

A429

N

0   1/2   1
Scale   One Mile

Link with Windrush Way

92 miles

Buckle Street

E

Houses

River Windrush

F

Aston Farm

Course of old Railway

93 miles

© Crown copyright

H B M △
BOURTON-ON-THE-WATER

SEE MAP 18

TO CIRENCESTER

(A) Cross the busy A436 with great care, through double metal gates and keep to left-hand edge of field with wall on immediate left. *Now traversing some classic 'Cotswold country', with rolling wolds and wide open views; and if its early summer, skylarks will almost certainly be singing above.* Pass attractive clump of trees over to left which are sited on top of a Stone Age long barrow or burial mound. Follow hedge-line as it curves down to right and then bear left through gap in wall, passing to left of old farm vehicles, to farm track with buildings of Camp Farm down to right. Turn left onto track and almost immediately turn right to follow up left-hand side of field with hedge to left. Through gap in hedge converging from right, still keeping to left-hand edge of field.

(B) Bear right onto minor road just beyond small wood on left. (We shall now follow road into Cold Aston, with its church soon visible over to right.) Down hill into valley with woods soon on both sides and up road, noting alternative name for this village on its entry sign - Aston Blank. *Having visited this high wold village in winter, we feel that its usual name 'Cold Aston' is totally justifiable!* Bear half-left at Cold Aston's village green with its massive sycamore tree, telephone box and delightful inn, the Plough; taking small road to immediate left of inn. *But go straight ahead if you wish to visit the interesting, largely Norman church, with pleasant stone vaulting beneath its tower.* Soon pass cottage on right called *Alberts* and over low stone stile at end of small road. Down narrow path with fence to left and wall to right, over second stile and turn right keeping fence on immediate right. Over third stile and through gate to pass in front of house with small ha-ha bordered lawn on right.

(C) Over fourth stile and bear left onto Bangup Lane, a surfaced track happily signed *Unfit for Motor Vehicles*, which we shall follow as far as Turkdean. Soon pass two houses on right, one known as Bangup Barn. After one-and-a-half miles go up attractive sunken road overhung with trees at entry to Turkdean.

(D) Turn left onto road by small triangular green in Turkdean and go through village. Pass *Old Shop* (B&B) on left, with telephone box just beyond. *On left pass church in large churchyard bordered by chestnut trees. The interior has several interesting features including a Norman chancel arch and a medieval stone pulpit.* Turn right where road bends to left beyond horse trough on right, onto sunken footpath overhung with trees which leads down hill. Soon enter hamlet of Lower Dean on track with house on left. Over small bridge crossing stream, pass post box on right and bear right onto road by house over to left (B&B). Up hill on road leaving Lower Dean, soon passing Castle Barn Farm on left and woods on right.

(E) Straight, not right at minor road junction (SP

Bangup Lane, well beyond Cold Aston

- *Hampnett*) and immediately **cross busy A40 with great care**, to join minor road (SP - *Hampnett village only*). Pass Hampnett entry sign and start to drop down into this minute village, its wide green having houses thinly spread around it. Through gate and keep on road through village, soon passing trough on left of road which is source of River Leach. *This flows south-eastwards from here to join the Thames just below Lechlade. The nearby, largely Norman church has an unusual interior decorated in 'medieval style' in the 1880s.* Turn right onto small road leading down hill by telephone box with church just beyond on left (SP - *No Through Road*). *(But go straight ahead, past church and then bear right onto path down valley if you wish to visit Northleach, with its Countryside Museum, Mechanical Music Museum and fine wool church - one mile).*

(F) Back on main route (having turned right) - bear left keeping on surfaced road where infant River Leach flows beneath it and almost immediately turn right onto path just before road becomes private drive. Up path with walls on both sides and through metal gate into field. Route is now straight ahead, but you must skirt around right-hand edge of field, keeping wall and fences to right (and not going through gate), and then down slope to go through small gate. Straight across field in deep valley aiming for stile just to left of junction of wall lines. Over stile and keep to immediate left of wall.

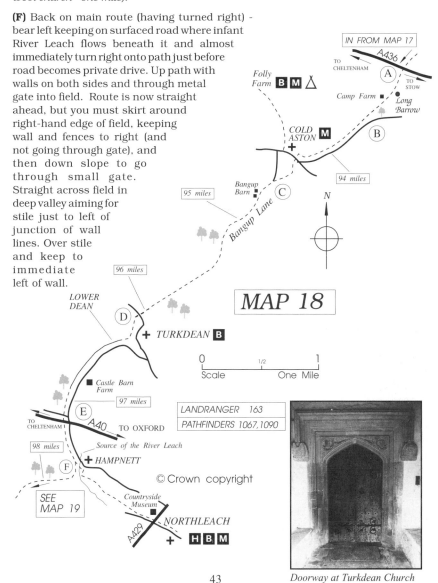

IN FROM MAP 17

A436

TO CHELTENHAM

TO STOW

Folly Farm **B** **M** △

Camp Farm ■

Long Barrow

COLD ASTON **M**

✚

94 miles

Bangup Barn ■

Bangup Lane

95 miles

N

96 miles

LOWER DEAN

✚ TURKDEAN **B**

MAP 18

0   1/2   1
Scale   One Mile

■ *Castle Barn Farm*

97 miles

TO CHELTENHAM

A40   TO OXFORD

98 miles

Source of the River Leach

✚ HAMPNETT

© Crown copyright

LANDRANGER   163
PATHFINDERS 1067, 1090

SEE MAP 19

Countryside Museum ■

✚ NORTHLEACH

A429

✚ **H B M**

Doorway at Turkdean Church

43

(A) Through wooden gate and go across busy minor road onto smaller road forking right (SP - Fossebridge). After about 50 yards turn right down track with mature plantation on right and young plantation on left. Turn left at end of young plantation and note stone leaning against wall on immediate left beyond bend in wall. *This is known locally as the Hangman's Stone, and it appears to have been named as such due to a sheep-stealer who accidentally hung himself while getting over a stile in this wall with a stolen sheep in his arms. A highly moral, but rather unlikely, story !* Now go into field keeping to immediate left of another young plantation on its right. Down field now keeping to immediate left of hedge and fence, soon veering slightly right and passing beneath electric power-line with large pylon just to right. Through gap in fence coming in from left into smaller field with large barns of Oxpens Farm on left. Soon turn left with fence and wall to immediate right and, just before reaching barns, turn right after stone wall.. Follow down between wall on right and fence with spinney on left and over stile. Go diagonally left across very small field.

(B) Soon turn right down well surfaced farm road and follow this down into valley. Cross stream, a tributary of River Coln and pass old, stone-lined sheep wash on right. Climb track up into farmyard, which marks our entry into Yanworth. Bend left and then right, following track through farmyard past attractive stone barns and, on right, delightful little Yanworth Church. *Here will be found a Norman south doorway, a chancel arch of the same period and a wall-painting of Old Father Time complete with his scythe.* Up surfaced road beyond church, turn left at top and almost immediately right onto road in village (SP - *Roman Villa*). Go through village, passing village hall on right, cast-iron water pump on left and delightful *Dolls' Cottage* and telephone box, both on right.

(C) Turn left at road junction (SP - *Fossebridge*) and go down road towards beautifully wooded Coln Valley. *Good view of fine Elizabethan mansion of Stowell Park well over to left.* Pass converted Yanworth Mill on right and, immediately

beyond bridge over River Coln, turn right where road bends to left. Now on broad surfaced track with extensive woodlands up to left and water meadows to right as we walk parallel with River Coln. Many pheasants in woods - please keep dogs on lead.

(D) After one mile pass cottage on left and after another 200 yards go through gate to turn left onto surfaced road (SP - *Roman Villa*). Up fairly steep slope, keeping on surfaced road and ignoring track to left. Soon pass the National Trust's Chedworth Roman Villa on right and go onto footpath to immediate left of National Trust reception building. *In an attractive woodland setting and dating from between AD 180 and AD 350, these very interesting and beautifully preserved remains include bath suites, a hypocaust and mosaic pavements. There is also a museum and shop, and a 9-minute introductory film provides a fascinating insight into life and work in the Romano-British countryside. Don't miss a visit here - you*

Woods beyond Chedworth Roman Villa

could even reward yourself with an ice cream! Go up steep, stony path through woods, soon disregarding steps up to left and going through underbridge beneath old railway embankment. After 100 yards, turn left at x-rds of tracks and continue to climb up through woods. Straight, not right at junction of tracks, going onto possibly muddier track. Fork right at Y-junction of tracks going gently up hill.

At Chedworth Roman Villa

(E) Over stile at end of wood and head straight across field to go to immediate right of fence coming in from left. Continue with fence now on immediate left, soon cross line of bridleway and through metal gate below sycamore tree. Go straight, not left, at next junction of paths and go steeply down through wood, initially on steps. Over stile at end of wood and keep in same direction across field in broad valley. Well concealed railway cutting beyond dense bushes to left, at southern end of old railway tunnel. Bear right near end of field and go over stile onto surfaced road at entry to Chedworth village. Soon pass church on right. *This light and airy building was considerably enriched in the Perpendicular period and has a stout Norman font, and, in contrast, an elegant 15th-century stone pulpit.* Keep on higher road (but bear left down path if you wish to visit the Seven Tuns, a welcoming inn with a spring bubbling out of a wall opposite). Pass attractive house and barn on right with pool in garden.

(F) Over first road and bear left up slope to left of village notice board. Immediately bear right across second road to go straight up track overhung with trees. After 100 yards, go straight over road onto track (SP -*Setts Farm House only*).

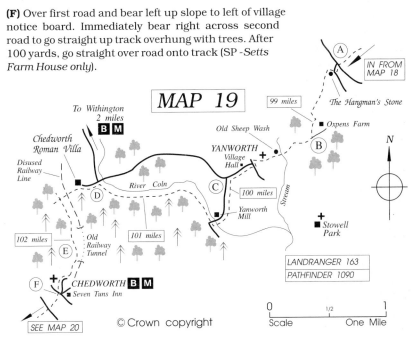

MAP 19

IN FROM MAP 18

The Hangman's Stone

99 miles

To Withington 2 miles **B** **M**

Old Sheep Wash

■ Oxpens Farm

Chedworth Roman Villa

YANWORTH Village Hall ■

B

N

Disused Railway Line

■

River Coln

C

100 miles

D

■ Yanworth Mill

Stream

102 miles

E

Old Railway Tunnel

101 miles

Stowell Park

F ✝ CHEDWORTH **B** **M**
Seven Tuns Inn

LANDRANGER 163
PATHFINDER 1090

© Crown copyright

0   1/2   1
Scale   One Mile

SEE MAP 20

45

(A) At Setts Farm House keep on track through double wooden gates, then through two single gates and stay on this with open views ahead. Pass end of hedgeline on left and keep straight along track, with view ahead of 'restored' World War I airfield, known as 'RFC Rendcomb' (Strictly private - do not try to visit). Through wide gap in wall now following hedge on left and dropping gently into shallow valley. After about 200 yards, keep on track, leaving theoretical right-of-way and onto permissive section (not signed as such). Bear right in bottom of valley, keeping on track and soon turn left at junction of tracks ignoring tree-lined track ahead.

(B) After about 300 yards turn right at junction of tracks, leaving permissive section and re-join right-of-way. Keep along broad track with open field on both

sides, gradually rising out of valley. Through gap at end of track and turn left onto road which follows course of minor Roman road known as the White Way. Cross this road onto small lane to left of waymark to Greenmeadow Farm. Follow lane passing narrow strip of wood to left. Fine views of Rendcomb ahead including its 'chateau-style' stable-block tower. Down lane and up short, steep hill.

(C) Soon pass footpath to left. *Use this if you wish to divert to Cirencester down Churn Valley - five-and-a-half miles. It would then be possible to re-join the main route at Tunnel House Inn (see page 49, Point H) - a further three-and three-quarter miles). There would*

Norman font at Rendcomb

therefore be no extra mileage involved, as the total distance of this major diversion is the same as that between its starting and finishing points on the main route. It is hoped to provide details of this diversion route in the Macmillan Way Planner, a supplement to this guide. Back on main route just before entry to Rendcomb - turn left at road junction (telephone phone box on left) by entry to estate village of Rendcomb, with Italianate Rendcomb Court used as boarding school. Pass Post Office shop and 'French-chateau-style' stable block (now school science building). Follow road to left. (But turn right if you wish to visit church.) *This was built by prosperous wool merchant, Sir Edmund Thame, son of the builder of better known Fairford church, with which it shares certain similarities. It also has a splendid Norman font.)* Follow road down hill, under bridge, cross infant River Churn and pass Rendcomb Surgery before reaching busy A435.

(D) Cross A435 with great care, going right and almost immediately left onto lane (SP - *Woodmancote*). Go up lane, looking back for good view of Rendcomb College. Go left through large wooden gate opposite cottage named *The Lodge* and just before large pylon. Go diagonally across field heading for left-hand end of dutch barn. Go through metal gate to immediate left of dutch barn and follow short fence on right before passing cottage. Immediately beyond cottage go over stile to right. Follow track to road into quiet hamlet of Woodmancote.

(E) Go left onto road in Woodmancote, telephone box soon on right by road junction. Bear right off road just beyond semi-detached house ('No 2') on right and before sign *North*

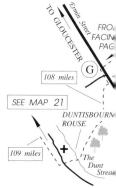

A hint of France at Rendcomb

Cerney and onto short, sunken bridleway. At end of this go slightly left across junction of surfaced drives, and then bear slightly right to go down lane passing just to right of Moor Wood, a large house with impressive gardens on both sides of lane. Go down lane and slightly right to pass Park Lodge stables with attractive cart-shed just beyond on right. Keep down rougher track with wood and stream on right.

(F) At fork of tracks where `Moorwood Estate - Strictly Private` sign is ahead, go left on track with hedge on left. Bend to left at valley bottom and climb up track with good views back across valley to Woodmancote, to pass coniferous wood on left. After one-third-of-a-mile go straight ahead on concrete drive towards house near Dartley Farm, but just before house go left onto tarmac lane leading to main road.

(G) Cross the busy A417 with very great care. *This follows the course of the Romans' Ermin Way, which ran from Silchester, near Reading, through Cirencester,*

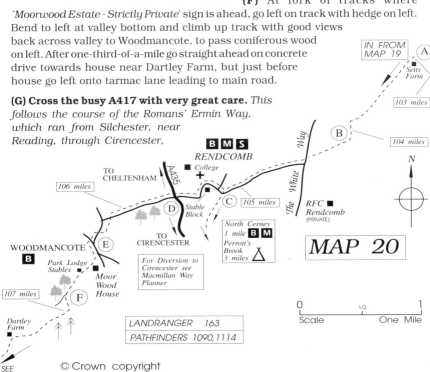

IN FROM MAP 19 — A

Setts Farm

103 miles

B — 104 miles

N

B M S
RENDCOMB
College

TO CHELTENHAM

106 miles

A435

D — Stable Block

C — 105 miles

The White Way

RFC — Rendcomb (PRIVATE)

TO CIRENCESTER

North Cerney
1 mile **B M**
Perrott's Brook
3 miles △

MAP 20

WOODMANCOTE — **B** — E

Park Lodge Stables

Moor Wood House

F

For Diversion to Cirencester see Macmillan Way Planner

107 miles

Dartley Farm

0 — 1/2 — 1
Scale — One Mile

LANDRANGER 163
PATHFINDERS 1090,1114

SEE FACING PAGE

© Crown copyright

to their legionary fortress at Gloucester. Still being very straight, it encourages driving that is far too fast. Go left along far verge of A417, ignoring entry to lane signed *Middle Duntisbourne* and after 100 yards turn right through hedge onto bridle-way. Follow wall and hedge on left for about 100 yards and turn left through metal gate in hedge. Go right with bushy hedge now on right and, after a while, through next metal gate keeping hedge on right. Good views ahead of Cirencester Park woodlands. Continue skirting edge of field before bearing off right down path between hedge on right and wood on left. Continue down sunken lane and go over small bridge to left of ford crossing the Dunt stream in pretty Duntisbourne Rouse hamlet.

(A) Go up short lane and turn right onto minor road (SP - *The Duntisbournes / Youth Hostel*). After 100 yards pass entry to exceptionally interesting Duntisbourne Rouse church on right - don't miss a visit. *This tiny Saxon church has a saddleback roof to its tower and an interior complete with box pews, carved misericords to its choir stalls and medieval wall paintings on its north chancel wall. Being built on a slope it has, most unusually, a little crypt beneath its eastern end.* After about 300 yards turn left onto bridleway. Go along bridleway and after 300 yards bear right by wooden barn on left and follow track to right.

(B) After three-quarters-of-a-mile, cross minor road and through wooden gate onto further bridleway, which skirts to right (north) of Overley Wood - the northern fringe of Cirencester Park's great woodlands. *Please note that almost all the way from here to the Tunnel House Inn (see opposite) is within Cirencester Park, part of the Bathurst Estate, and to meet this estate's requirements, Macmillan Way waymarks will unfortunately not be displayed. However, the route is well signed with standard waymarks and little difficulty should be experienced.* At end of bridleway turn left onto minor road and pass Gloucester Lodge on left - this is one of the northern entrances to Cirencester Park. Continue southwards on minor road.

(C) Immediately after passing signed entrance to Pinbury Park (private) turn right onto bridleway and immediately right again through hunting gate. Follow an indistinct path on immediate right of hawthorn hedge and parallel with private road to Pinbury Park on right. Veer to left as bridleway drops down to run close to private road. Soon leave private road and skirt to left of pond, going between pond and its feeding spring. Through double gates just beyond pond and follow field path south-westwards aiming between two power-poles. *Lovely 17th-century Pinbury Park (house) visible back across valley to right.*

(D) Through gate into bushy area and at junction of tracks just beyond, carry straight ahead, slightly up hill, ignoring path to left. Continue south-westwards on path in middle of delightful meadow ringed by fine trees. Through gate keeping on path to left of fence with view of house called *The Leasowes* to right. Continuing left, pass through small gate and turn right onto well defined bridleway. Through gate and bear half-left to cross field to telephone box in Sapperton village. *Sapperton church is over to right and is approached up a path below yew trees. In the north transept of this largely 18th-century building, Sir Henry Poole, who died in 1616, lies in a great canopied Renaissance tomb, with many effigies. Adjacent to it is another Poole tomb dated 1574. In the south transept Sir Robert Atkyns, who died in 1711, lies on his left elbow with his hand resting upon a book. He was the county historian and wrote 'The Ancient and Present State of Gloucestershire'. Trim and colourful Sapperton is very much a Bathurst estate village and below it runs the tunnel of the two-and-a-quarter-mile-long Thames and Severn Canal (see page 50), the western portal of which is at Daneway in the valley below Sapperton.*

Duntisbourne Rouse Church

(E) Back on main route - turn left up hill near telephone box, soon passing the Bell Inn on left and bus stop. Turn right at road junction (SP - *Cherington*) and soon cross 'The Sapperton Broad Avenue', *a broad grassy ride, also known as 'The Broad Ride', which runs eastwards for nearly five miles to Cirencester, with only a short break in open country around Pope's Seat. A notice states 'You are welcome on horseback or on foot along the Sapperton Broad Avenue. Please keep dogs on leads'. It should be noted however* *that this facility applies only between 8 am and 5pm.*

(F) Soon turn left at x-rds (SP - *Cirencester*). Go along road, with view to right of one of the spoil heaps created by the excavators of the tunnel for the Thames and Severn Canal. Ignore first bridleway fingerpost to right and **proceed with great care along this often busy minor road** until a plantation joins our road on left. At this point turn right, off road and through gap in stone wall. Cross field, through large metal gates and **cross busy A419 with great care** to go through large metal gates. Continue in same direction across field noting another tunnel spoil heap over to right.

(G) At end of field go through gate into Hailey Wood and continue ahead veering slightly left on track to plunge into this very large wood. Continue on track ignoring other, crossing rides and paths and approximately following the course of canal tunnel beneath. *Note spoil heap to right with exposed air shaft, but keep away from fenced edge - it could be very dangerous). Like the rest, this shaft was first used to extract spoil from the tunnel beneath and was then used for ventilation.* After about 500 yards veer slightly to left and soon go straight across wide track which descends from estate saw-mill up to left (not visible) and which also goes to right, over embankment, with parapet of railway bridge just visible beyond. Continue on footpath, then turn half-right at junction with track coming in from left. Go under railway line, turn left and follow path running parallel with railway, and pass through gate before reaching vicinity of Tunnel House Inn.

(H) *We are joined here by the diversion route from Rendcomb via Cirencester (see page 46, Point C).*

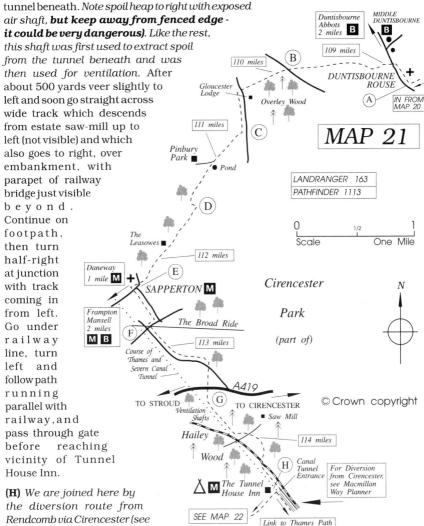

Duntisbourne Abbots 2 miles **B**

MIDDLE DUNTISBOURNE **B**

109 miles

110 miles

B

DUNTISBOURNE ROUSE

Gloucester Lodge

Overley Wood

A

IN FROM MAP 20

111 miles

C

MAP 21

Pinbury Park

Pond

LANDRANGER 163

PATHFINDER 1113

D

0   1/2   1

Scale   One Mile

The Leasowes

112 miles

Daneway 1 mile **M**

E

SAPPERTON **M**

Cirencester

N

Frampton Mansell 2 miles **M B**

F

The Broad Ride

Park

113 miles

(part of)

Course of Thames and Severn Canal Tunnel

A419

© Crown copyright

TO STROUD

G

TO CIRENCESTER

Ventilation Shafts

Saw Mill

Hailey

114 miles

Wood

H

Canal Tunnel Entrance

M The Tunnel House Inn

For Diversion from Cirencester, see Macmillan Way Planner

SEE MAP 22

Link to Thames Path (See Map 22)

Chapter 5 Tunnel House Inn, Coates -
Bradford-on-Avon   37 Miles

(A) Bear right, across car parking area in front of Tunnel House Inn and go past old cider press on left, making for gap in wall. *(However, follow towpath along bank of partly restored Thames and Severn Canal if you wish to link onto the Thames Path at Thames Head, the source of the Thames, which is about a mile away.)* The Tunnel House Inn was built to house, feed and especially water, the navvies who dug the canal tunnel and the thirsty boatmen who used it when completed. The tunnel, the delightful portal of which is still visible near the inn, was completed in 1789 and was, at that time, the longest canal tunnel in England. It enabled boats to cross the Cotswolds from the head of the navigable Thames at Lechlade to the Severn via the Stroudwater Canal. Sadly it was finally abandoned in 1927. Now an attractive and welcoming pub, the Tunnel House is full of curiosities and delights.

(B) Now back on main route beyond Tunnel House Inn, having gone through gap in wall beyond cider press. Go along wide footpath through field, *with slight earthworks of Roman 'settlement' sometimes visible over to left. Now known as Tunnel Mouth Camp it was probably a religious complex dating from the 3rd or 4th century AD, but it has never been systematically excavated (Do not Trespass).* Over stone stile in wall into next field and now follow line of power-poles, which presently leads towards stile in dry stone wall on right. Over this stile and up across next field to go over wooden stile. Go diagonally right, across field to fingerpost and through metal gate near small house in Tarlton.

(C) At entry to Tarlton, *a minute village with a number of pleasant houses and a small neo-Norman church,* go slightly left, cross road and turn right onto well surfaced track leading through farmyard. Pass fine old barns on right and walk through farmyard to leave Tarlton on track beyond farm cottages on right. Bear slightly left keeping on farm track and after about half-a-mile, at end of track, go through metal gate into field. Turn half right to cross corner of field and through second metal gate. Keep in same direction across corner of next field to go through third metal gate and across larger field to go through wooden gate into scrubby woodland. Now veer slightly left to follow short track.

(D) Soon turn left onto surfaced track and head south-westwards with woodlands to left. After about 600 yards go straight ahead to join minor road. After about 50 yards go straight ahead onto track where road turns left. After just over half a mile cross minor road and through wooden gate onto further track in same direction.

(E) After about 350 yards and at first wall-line to right, turn right through old, small gateway *(now on permissive path - 'Private' notice states MWO - Macmillan Way Only)* and go up right-hand side of field keeping wall on immediate right. At end of field bear slightly right through gap and bear slightly left joining farm track. Drop down on track bearing left at bottom with good view of delightful 16th- and 17th-century Hazleton Manor over to left. Bear left at junction of tracks and keep on track out of small valley (do not go through gates into field to right). Now bear right, then left, with barns to left. Turn right just beyond transformer

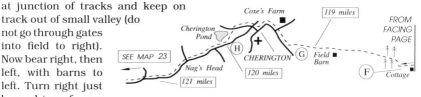

SEE MAP 23

Coxe's Farm

119 miles

FROM FACING PAGE

Cherington Pond

CHERINGTON

Field Barn

Nag's Head

120 miles

121 miles

Cottage

East Portal of the Thames and Severn Canal Tunnel

on pole to left *(re-joining normal right-of-way)* and go straight along farm road to Shepherd's Cottages.

(F) At end of farm road go straight across field to gate. Through this gate into wood and after about 20 yards, fork right along waymarked pathway (yellow arrows only). Soon bear left and after going along narrow path, emerge at end of wood. Now go across five fields in a straight line, passing Field Barn on left and keeping to immediate left of hedgelines where they exist.

(G) Over stile beside metal gate, bear right onto public road and go straight, not right by Coxe's Farm at entry to Cherington village (SP - *Avening*). Turn right (SP - *Avening*) by pleasant green *overlooked by several pleasant 18th and early 19th-century cottages, with an ancient wellhead on it, inscribed, 'Let Him that is athirst, come'. The nearby church is largely 13th-century in origin and has a Norman south doorway with tympanum, a Norman tub font and a list of rectors, curates and patrons dating back to 1287.* Just beyond village, go over diagonal x-rds roads on hill (SP - *Stroud*) and **go down steep hill with care**. At bottom of hill bear left off road by parking space and through wooden gate. Keep on often muddy path with stream on right and then pass delightful lake on right, known as Cherington Pond. At end of lake bear left up slight incline.

(H) Soon through small wooden gate and bear right onto minor road. Keep on road through hamlet of Nag's Head (the pub has gone long ago), keeping straight, not right by telephone box. After 500 yards go straight, not left and after further 300 yards, turn left onto busier road into Avening village (SP - *Tetbury*).

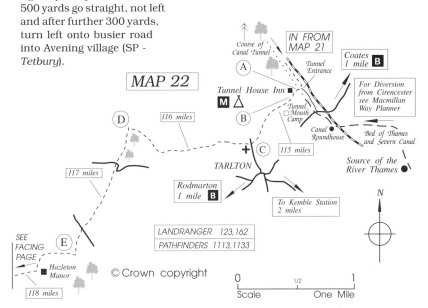

IN FROM MAP 21

Course of Canal Tunnel

MAP 22

Coates 1 mile **B**

Tunnel Entrance

Tunnel House Inn ■ **M** △

Tunnel Mouth Camp

For Diversion from Cirencester see Macmillan Way Planner

(A)

(B)

(D)

116 miles

(C) 115 miles

+

TARLTON

Canal Roundhouse

Bed of Thames and Severn Canal

Source of the River Thames ●

117 miles

Rodmarton 1 mile **B**

To Kemble Station 2 miles

N

SEE FACING PAGE

(E)

Hazleton Manor

118 miles

© Crown copyright

LANDRANGER   123,162
PATHFINDERS 1113,1133

0   1/2   1
Scale   One Mile

(A) After 200 yards pass Cross Inn on left and go straight onto B4014 (SP - *Nailsworth*), passing small general stores on left. After 200 yards bear left up Point Road by telephone box. Soon keep straight, **not** left up Pound Hill, but descend, with good view of Avening church down to right and then bear left at T-junction and up hill, still on Point Road. Straight, not left at road junction by de-restriction signs (SP - *West End*) and just beyond, turn left through large wooden gate, up a steep grassy footpath. Over stile (good views back over valley to Gatcombe Park) and walk as near as possible to right-hand edge of field. Keep to right of small spinney near right-hand corner of field and over stone stile. Follow wall to left soon passing fine farmhouse on left with clock tower.

(B) Over stile to left of metal gate, cross surfaced farm drive and along next field keeping wall on left. Over rudimentary stile and continue with wall still on left, but before end of field, bear left over massive stone stile and go diagonally left across field aiming for far left-hand corner just to left of clump of trees.. Go through gap, turn left through second gap and immediately right onto B4014 road. Go along road and after 200 yards, at first gentle bend to left, bear right through gap. Then turn left into spinney and immediately go diagonally right aiming just to left of pylon, and then for waymark. Over stone stile, cross minor road and over rudimentary stile in wall. Go diagonally right, across field aiming for wall heading straight towards you at far side. Through large gap in cross-hedge and into next field keeping to immediate right of parallel wall. Over rudimentary stile in left-hand end of cross-fence near end of field.

(C) Soon go through gate to cross minor road. *(But walk about 100 yards down road to left for glimpse of Chavenage House through its entrance gates). Chavenage is a delightful Elizabethan manor house, which was once visited by Oliver Cromwell, to persuade the owner, Colonel Nathaniel Stephens, to put his name to Charles I's Death Warrant. The colonel grudgingly agreed, but then died within three months of the king's execution, apparently full of remorse.*

(C) On main route - over road going slightly right, onto farm road with asbestos barn to right and old stone barn to left. Bear slightly left down sometimes muddy bridleway (known as Chavenage Lane) going between walls, soon passing wood on left, rich with bluebells in late spring. At end of wood, go down bridleway bordered by hedges and trees.

(D) Through gate, bear down left and through another gate at bottom of small valley. *If you wish to divert to Tetbury for overnight stop, fork left onto footpath along valley, turn right onto road, then fork left at road junction and soon enter Tetbury - about two miles. This unspoilt little market town is centred upon its delightful 17th-century Market House and the nearby church of St Mary. This has a slim tower and spire, and an elegant and beautifully proportioned late-17th-century interior. But in addition to these main features, Tetbury has a wealth of interesting old buildings and is well worth visiting. To return to main route - leave centre of town on Church Street, turn right into West Street, opposite church and then bear left down Cotton's Lane.*

Soon turn left onto Cutwell and cross River Avon on small stone bridge beside ford. Turn right onto Longfurlong Lane and leave town on this, keeping straight not right well beyond. At end of Longfurlong Lane, go through two gates in front of Elmestree Lodge. Go diagonally left across fields and parkland in front of Elmestree House following waymarks. Slight hint of Highgrove House over to left. Then into field with hedge on left before going

on grassy gallop for short distance. Then bear left over stile through hedge and follow in same direction along three fields, keeping to immediate left of hedge-line. Now over final stile and re-join main route at Point G (see below) by turning left onto Hookshouse Lane, some 400 yards north of diagonal x-rds near Westonbirt. (Distance from Tetbury under three miles)

(D) Back on main route, in valley beyond Chavenage. Aim slightly left and go up slope with fence and bushes to right, with good view back to Chavenage House. Through large metal gate at top of slope and continue on bridleway with hedge to right. Fine distant views to left of Tetbury with its splendid, tall-spired church. Continue on bridleway with good views of Beverston Castle over to right before reaching A4135.

(E) Turn right onto often busy A4135 and almost immediately turn left off it through hunting gate beside large metal gates. *(But follow road westwards for half-a-mile if you wish to visit Beverston. The church in this small village has an unusual Anglo-Saxon sculpture on its tower and some interesting features within. Beverston Castle, one of the few surviving Cotswold castles, is nearby, a largely 13th-century building with 17th-century additions. It is not open but glimpses can be obtained from the road.)* On main route - follow broad and grassy bridleway, eventually going onto more defined track with trees and fences on both sides, and into small valley. Up track beyond it and through field before going through gate and bearing right at Hookshouse hamlet.

(F) Almost immediately fork left at road junction by interesting Hookshouse Pottery on right (SP - *Westonbirt*). Follow Hookshouse Lane southwards passing Charlton Down (house) on left.

(G) After about half-a-mile pass footpath sign on left *(this is where diversion route from Tetbury rejoins main route)*. Distant view over to right of elegant pavilion of the Beaufort Polo Club).

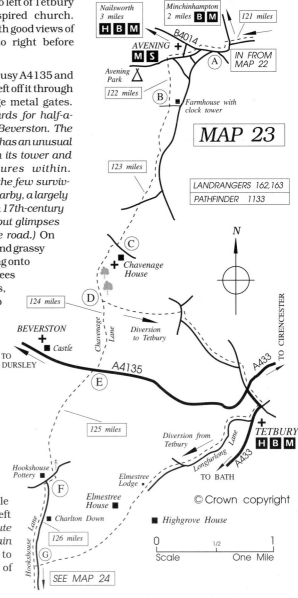

53

(A) At diagonal x-rds turn right over stile and along field with wall on immediate right. Through gate and keep to left-hand edge of field with northern edge of Westonbirt Arboretum to left - occasional vistas of tall and exotic trees, undulating lawns, leisurely seats and arbours. Through gate into next field, still following wall on left. Down Farm visible over to right with the Beaufort Polo Club's pavilion to its immediate right. Through offset gap in wooden fence and through two more gates continuing on same line.

(B) Just before spinney, visible ahead, go through gate on left into Arboretum's field. Descend this field on sunken cart track, then veer slightly right in small valley and go over squeeze stile (ignoring standard waymarks) on edge of wood (now on a Permissive Path). *But turn left down valley and purchase entry tickets at far end of car park if you wish to leave course of Macmillan Way and visit rest of Arboretum, with its Visitor Centre, cafe and shop.) Westonbirt Arboretum was the creation of Sir Robert Holford, the owner of nearby neo-Elizabethan Westonbirt House, which is now a school. This world famous collection of over 13,000 trees stands in a beautiful 600-acre landscape with woodland paths and grassy glades. It has been owned by the Forestry Commission since 1956.* Back on main route - over squeeze stile into Westonbirt Arboretum's Silk Wood and bear slightly to right before going up slope. Follow path and then turn left onto bridleway, re-joining right-of-way, which leads to the Broad Drive.

(C) Continue in same direction down the Broad Drive - main north-south axis of the Silk Wood - noting fine trees with their helpful placards. Continue in same direction, ignoring paths to left and right and aiming for large gate in distance. Go through hunting gate beside large gate, which marks southern extremity of Silk Wood *(but turn right (SP - Willow Collection), along path just within wood if you wish to go to Avenue Farm for B&B).* On main route, cross field keeping to immediate left of hedge.

(D) Through metal gate, **cross busy A433 with great care**, passing from Gloucestershire into Wiltshire and going onto wide track (Wood Lane) between house on left and kennels on right (beware of dog droppings). Through gate into next field keeping hedge on immediate left. Tower of Sherston church already visible well ahead, with distant Marlborough Downs on skyline well to its left. Follow path to end of field and through gate to cross very narrow field with barn to right. Soon pass beneath ash trees and into next field keeping on track with hedge to immediate right.

(E) Through gate at end of field and continue in same direction down road. Soon pass Halfway Bush Farm on right and 500 yards beyond, go through gate on left. Go diagonally right, across field to far corner aiming for farm buildings well beyond. Bear right in corner through metal gate and along left-hand edge of field with hedge and wall on left. Through gap in cross hedge and continue in same line with hedge still on left. At end of field go straight ahead onto wide track with hedge on left and wall on right. Sherston visible over to right and house to left.

(F) Turn right onto road but immediately over stile and cross field to kissing gate in wall with Sherston church tower visible ahead. Through kissing gate and follow well used path to another kissing gate. Up driveway with

Path in the Silk Wood, Westonbirt Arboretum

54

houses on right and wall on left at entry to Sherston and bear right onto B4040. *A large village with wide main street, Sherston was a borough by the 15th century and the variety of beautiful stone houses and inns still bear witness to its past prosperity. Only just over the border into Wiltshire, but it already seems to have a slightly 'West Country' flavour, with several inns offering food and a number of shops. Its church has a handsomely vaulted Perpendicular porch and a stout tower, surprisingly built as late as 1730.* Walk through Sherston on B4040, passing Carpenters Arms on left and church on right. Pass Rattlebone Inn on left, Post Office on right and phone box on left. After passing Platts Stores on left, **take care when walking down steep road with dangerously blind bend**.

(G) Soon cross infant River Avon *(this one flows into the Bristol Channel at Avonmouth)* and immediately beyond, go over stone stile on left (SP - *The Grove*). *In the event of flooding in field ahead, turnabout, soon fork right and take first four turns to right, to use minor roads to rejoin route near Convery Ciders - see below.* On main route - bear right beyond stile aiming for bridge in field. Over bridge crossing tributary of River Avon, continue in same direction with stream now on right and wooded area known as 'The Grove' to left. Over stile and go straight across very small field dotted with scrub. Soon over another stile and into large open terraced field. Go along terrace but before end of field veer up left just before power-pole and up onto top terrace to go over high stone stile in left-hand corner. Veer slightly left and head for waymark post soon visible across field.

(H) Over stile in wall and turn right onto road. Pass sign to Convery Ciders and Wines on left and soon over raised path beside ford at entry to Brook End hamlet. After houses on both sides, turn left at offset x-rds (SP - *No Through Road*) to go down small lane with pleasant old houses on both sides. Go along raised path beside another ford (on left) before going on gravel track.

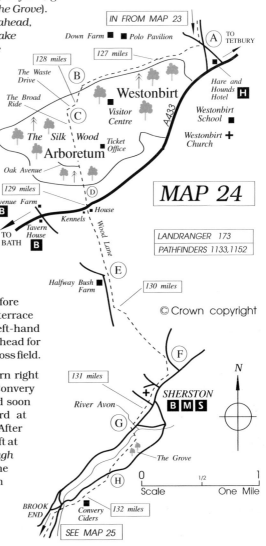

IN FROM MAP 23

Down Farm ■   ■ Polo Pavilion

A   TO TETBURY

128 miles

127 miles

The Waste Drive   B

The Broad Ride

Westonbirt

Hare and Hounds Hotel   H

Westonbirt School ■

C

Visitor Centre

The Silk Wood

Arboretum

Ticket Office

Westonbirt Church ✝

A433

Oak Avenue

129 miles   D

Avenue Farm   B   ■ House

Kennels

TO BATH   Tavern House   B

Wood Lane

MAP 24

LANDRANGER 173
PATHFINDERS 1133,1152

Halfway Bush Farm   E

130 miles

© Crown copyright

F

N

131 miles

River Avon

SHERSTON
B M S

✝

G

The Grove

H

0   1/2   1
Scale   One Mile

BROOK END

Convery Ciders   132 miles

SEE MAP 25

55

(A) Bear up right towards stable yard at entry to Luckington, but just before entrance gates with small lions, go through gap in wall to their left and onto path through churchyard, keeping to right of church and noting signs warning of falling masonry. *The church is a modest building of 13th-century origin with some handsome 18th-century tomb chests in its churchyard. It has a delightful neighbour in Luckington Court, a mellow and beautifully proportioned Queen Anne house.* Through front gate of churchyard onto tarmac path leading to another gate onto road. Turn right onto road, immediately pass entrance to Luckington Court on right and after a few yards turn left and over stile onto path between two houses *(but go straight ahead up road if you wish to visit the Old Royal Ship Inn, or village shop)*. Soon over stile into field, first following hedge on right and then diagonally right aiming for electricity pole and going through gap in hedge. Now bear left to go diagonally to far bottom corner of field. Over wooden stile and follow winding path down into more wooded area. Over bridge crossing stream and turn right to go along valley bottom, with willow-bordered stream now to right, and head for gate.

(B) Through gate, turn right onto minor road. Immediately before road junction, turn left off road and go over small stile in wall to left of gate. Go up grounds of bungalow keeping close to wall on left and to left of two outbuildings. Over stile into small paddock and over second stile into large field. Continue in same line (southwards) keeping to left-hand edge of field with hedge on left. Go through very wide gap in partial cross hedge.

(C) Continue into field in same direction for about 200 yards before veering right (south-westwards) to aim for ash tree in middle of facing hedge. Through gap in hedge to right of ash tree and continue in same direction, diagonally across next field aiming for far right-hand top corner. Keep to immediate left of small triangular plantation and near corner of field through squeeze-stile in thick hedge. Keeping in same direction, go diagonally left across small field aiming for waymarked stile in hedge. Over this stile and go across next field passing well to left of small pond (with Hebden Farm visible over to right) to go through large metal gate. Note old brick-kiln over to right just beyond small house.

(D) Bear left beyond gate (now southwards) aiming to left of bushes which surround a larger, partly concealed, pond. Through gateway to left of pond and veer slightly right aiming for point between two oaks in valley. Soon over two small concrete 'bridges' and through underbridge in railway embankment carrying busy Swindon - Bristol line **(Do not attempt to cross railway line, which is used by many very fast trains)**. Now head up towards lone oak tree in large meadow and then to right-hand end of wood on left.

(E) Through gateway at end of wood on left and veer slightly left aiming for gate well to left of woodlands ahead. *This field marks our only incursion into the County of Avon.* Through gate, returning to Wiltshire, and veer left to cross small part of field aiming for gap which lies to left of sight-line to church tower ahead. Through

Remains of Lugbury Long Barrow

gap in hedge and continue in same direction now aiming for gateway with house well beyond it. Through gateway and bear diagonally right across field towards gate in hedge ahead. Through gate, bear right onto road and soon bear left at road junction near entry to small village of Littleton Drew, which has no shop or inn. *Its church has a slender Perpendicular tower and in the porch are two large pieces of a 9th-century Saxon cross.* Go straight through village passing telephone box and church on right and ignoring footpath signs.

(F) Follow road out of village, going straight, not left at road junction just beyond and soon beneath noisy M4 motorway to arrive at T-junction. Cross busy B4039 with great care and go to left of small shed, straight down narrow surfaced lane (SP - *No Through Road*). Pass Goulter's Mill Farm on right (B & B), then bear left passing cart-shed on left before crossing bridge over By Brook *(we shall soon rejoin this stream and follow it until reaching Box - see page 60).* Bear left beyond bridge, through metal gate and soon bear right, following track up hill to right of beech plantation. Through metal gate at end of plantation and keep straight up right-hand edge of field with wall to right. Through hunting gate at top of field and keep straight along right-hand edge of field with hedge on right. *Note Lugbury Long Barrow over to left, with the great stones of its main chambered tomb exposed on its top. Described by the 17th-century antiquary, John Aubrey, as 'a great Table stone of bastard freestone leaning on two pitched perpendicular stones', it is still impressive today. Constructed in Neolithic times it must already have been over two thousand years old when the Roman legionaries were building the nearby Fosse Way.* Bear right beyond small spinney and go through two metal hunting gates. Follow to immediate right of stone wall and after veering left, through large metal gate and keep on track to immediate right of wall.

(G) Through large metal gate and turn left onto road. Follow this road and over small x-rds crossing the Fosse Way (see page 40) (SP - *Nettleton*). *(But turn right if you wish to visit Stables Tea Room or Fosse Farm Country Hotel - visible from here.)* Keep down sunken lane, passing golf course on left, then over ladder stile beside gate and go quietly between houses at Nettleton Mill.

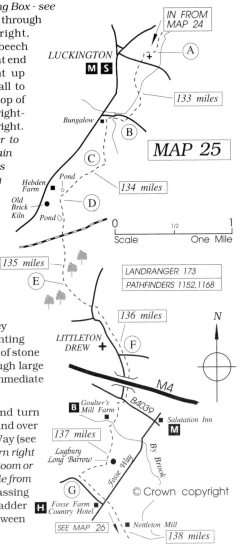

IN FROM MAP 24

LUCKINGTON **M** **S**

A

133 miles

Bungalow

B

C

MAP 25

Pond

Hebden Farm

134 miles

Old Brick Kiln

Pond

D

0   1/2   1
Scale   One Mile

135 miles

E

LANDRANGER 173

PATHFINDERS 1152, 1168

136 miles

N

LITTLETON DREW

F

M4

B Goulter's Mill Farm

B4039

■ Salutation Inn
M

137 miles

Lugbury Long Barrow

By Brook

Fosse Way

G

H Fosse Farm Country Hotel

SEE MAP 26

■ Nettleton Mill

138 miles

57

Houses near the Market Cross, Castle Combe

(A) Through concealed kissing gate to right of wrought-iron gate and bear left onto tree-shaded, surfaced path with pretty tributary stream alongside on left. Soon over stile and emerge onto golf course where we turn right and go on well surfaced path, keeping eye open for stray golf-balls and virtually silent golf-trolleys. Cross By Brook over attractive neo-Gothic stone bridge and immediately turn right onto less well surfaced path. Manor House Hotel visible down valley to right. Soon fork left going slightly uphill, leave golf course and go up path, bearing left, with wall on right and woods up to left. Turn right through squeeze-stile and down stone steps with walls on both sides. Under small stone bridge and soon onto surfaced driveway leading into Castle Combe.

(B) Under bridged gap between two houses. *This gap frames a delightful view of the Market Cross and the many old buildings surrounding it. Castle Combe lies snugly in the wooded valley of the little By Brook, with several fine old buildings around its little Market Cross reminding us of wealth once generated here by cloth weavers. The substantial tower of the largely Perpendicular church was built in 1434 'at the expense of the clothiers of the district', and the church's interior is well worth visiting.* Pass Castle Inn on left and church over to right before bearing right by Market Cross onto busier road with White Hart Inn opposite. Pass Post Office shop on left and over attractive stone bridge crossing By Brook. *It was in 1966 that the streamside down to the left was temporarily transformed by the producers of the film* Dr Doolittle *into a tiny 'harbour' complete with boats and jetty, a move not universally popular at the time.*

(C) Beyond end of village, turn left to cross small stone bridge over By Brook and immediately bear right onto well used path (SP - *Long Dean*). Over stone stile and bear up path to left into 'Conservation Area'. Now on slope with stream down to right, trees above to left and pools soon visible to right. Along path partly overhung with trees and bushes and into woodlands - fairly muddy in wet weather. Eventually go over stile across wall by gate and start to descend track with entry to sewage works on right (not very apparent).

(D) Enter pretty stone hamlet of Long Dean in its quiet, wooded valley, bearing right over small bridge and right again by Nut Tree Cottage up to left. Leave hamlet on track, cross bridge over By Brook ignoring waymark to left. Bear right at end of track by last house in hamlet and up steep, sunken path through woods. Through gate at end of woods and keep on well defined path with overhanging hedge to immediate right. Good views across valley to left. At gap in bushes, where main path bears to right, fork left following well defined path across slope of field and aiming for woods at far left-hand top end. Over stile and turn left onto road. Follow this narrow sunken road **with great care** down hill through woodlands, keeping on right-hand to face oncoming traffic.

(E) Bear right onto busy A420 (SP - *Bristol*) at entry to village of Ford. Pass bus shelter on right. Almost immediately **cross A420 with care** and turn left onto minor road (SP - *Colerne*). Pass White Hart Inn on left, go straight, not left just beyond, and at end of village, beyond house called *Tredena* on right, turn left over stile. Go over field keeping fence and trees on immediate left with small stream soon joining By Brook. Now veer right keeping By Brook, with its fishermen's benches, on left. Bear left, over footbridge crossing attractive By Brook above weir and over stone stile immediately beyond. Bear left by end of weir, following path along foot of woods to left and aim for stile in middle of fence ahead. Bear diagonally left to aim for gate in left-hand corner of field.

(F) Through metal gate, go over road at T-junction and over stile almost opposite. Go to left of Slaughterford's churchyard wall. Pass gate to churchyard on right. *The church with its pleasant tower lay derelict for nearly 200 years, having apparently been greatly damaged by Cromwell's troops when on their way to Ireland. It was rebuilt in 1883 and its interior still has a Victorian flavour. The small village just beyond lies quietly in the deep, wooded valley of the By Brook.* Go straight down to gate beyond churchyard to bear left onto pathway above road. Pass village seat and attractive cottages on left. Bear left keeping on road with By Brook now on immediate right. Bear left onto narrow road just before bridge on right (SP - *Weight limit 7.5 tonnes*). Bear right keeping on road overhung with trees (ignoring footpath and bridleway fingerposts).

(G) Straight, not left, at road junction at end of woods and onto Weavern Lane which is surfaced in its initial stages. Go straight across keeping on lane (SP - *Unsuitable for Motors*) (lane up to left leads to Honeybrook Farm). Weavern Lane now overhung with trees and likely to be muddy in winter. At start of Husseyhill Wood, with its attractive coppice plantations, go straight across at junction of tracks, ignoring waymark to left.

IN FROM MAP 25

Nettleton Mill

Neo-Gothic Bridge

Golf Course

138 miles Ⓐ

139 miles

Ⓑ

Manor House Hotel

CASTLE COMBE Ⓒ

H B M S

By Brook

140 miles

Ⓓ

MAP 26

To Fosseway Farm 2 miles

FORD

Long Dean

TO BRISTOL

A420

H

TO CHIPPENHAM

N

141 miles

Ⓔ

By Brook

Ⓕ

SLAUGHTERFORD

142 miles

Ⓖ

To Biddestone 1 mile

B M

0   1/2   1

Scale   One Mile

© Crown copyright

Weavern Lane

Honeybrook Farm

Husseyhill Wood

SEE MAP 27

143 miles

LANDRANGER 173
PATHFINDER 1168

59

(A) After about half-a-mile turn left, keeping on track which soon becomes much narrower, with overhanging bushes. After 250 yards turn right off lane by oak trees and through metal gate. Go down narrow bridleway into more open country with hedge on right and fence on left. At end of field go down sunken path with hedge to left and fence to right. Through small wooden gate and down path with fence still on right. Cross track at end of short field, through small wooden gate and pass notice stating 'No swimming'. Cross small stream with ruins of Weavern Farm over to right and fences on both sides of path.

(B) Over stone bridge crossing now substantial By Brook and through small wooden gate going up slope. Along path with Tilley's Wood just to right and fence to left. Pleasant views to left of By Brook and Hungerford Woods on slopes beyond. Through small wooden gate following well marked path across field with By Brook down to left and bushes and trees to right. Through small wooden gate to left of metal gate with By Brook just below to left. Go across field and eventually pass Widdenham Farmhouse on left before going through large wooden gate on to surfaced driveway.

(C) Onto road passing Widdenham Farm's farmyard and cottages on right and soon go straight ahead through large metal gate where road goes to right. Cross large field following path running approximately parallel with By Brook. Through small gate with By Brook now on immediate left and through field with By Brook still on left, heading for metal gate with farmhouse just beyond.

(D) Over stile beside metal gate and bear left onto road passing Saltbox Farm on right (B&B). Bear right at road junction beyond Saltbox Farm and up slight incline before turning left to go over stile. Follow left-hand hedge for short distance, then through narrow gap and bear right on well used path to cross large field keeping just to right of bend of By Brook. Spire of Box church visible well ahead, above waters of stream. Through narrow gap in cross-hedge just to right of By Brook and keep beside this stream, with its rushes and ducks, passing a few gardens on slopes beyond. Over stile in fence and immediately turn right by small weir, with fence on right. Bear left, with part of now divided stream on left, onto well surfaced path. Over footbridge onto wood-chipping path and bear left over attractive arched footbridge. Now turn right with By Brook on immediate right and fence on left. Box Mill (now a theatre) over to left.

(E) Bear left with care onto road entering village of Box. Pass Box Mill on left and under busy railway line before taking **second** of two footpaths to right, initially down a surfaced roadway alongside house (watch for this with care). *From here we shall start to steadily climb out of valley all the way to high ground beyond Henley.* At end of roadway go diagonally left across sports field keeping

Path beside the By Brook, approaching Saltbox Farm

off sensitive pitches and heading for point between cricket pavilion to left and tennis courts to right. Then bear left up roadway and, **with great care**, turn right onto busy A4 using footpath on far side. *Situated above the valley of the By Brook, the substantial village of Box has a number of handsome stone houses, the great quarries here having supplied much of the stone used by the builders of its elegant, much larger neighbour, Bath. The long Box Tunnel was one of the great features of Brunel's Great Western railway line from London to Bristol and the south aisle of Box Church was specially built for the use of his great gang of navvies. Do not miss the Blind House, a quaint little village lockup to our left, along the north side of the A4.*

(F) Go a few yards along A4 and then turn left just before Jacob Baylay's Ale House on right, to go up narrow, stepped footpath between houses. Now cross A365 with care and go up narrow steps onto pathway between two walls (SP - *Public Footpath Henley*). Cross driveway and then over two stiles passing nursery on right. Up across field with fence to immediate right, over another stile and go in same direction across meadow full of wild flowers. *Look back from here for fine views northwards up the valley of the By Brook.* Over stile beside metal gate and up another field keeping hedge and then wall on right, soon joining rough track. Pass Henley Farm on right, with its fine old stone barn. Over small stile and bear right onto road in hamlet of Henley. Turn left at road junction and follow road out of Henley. Turn left by grassy triangle onto slightly busier road and into hamlet of Blue Vein. Pass houses on right and also track on right signed *This is not a right-of-way,* but soon turn sharp right onto busier road.

(G) Pass sign on right - *Longsplatt* - and soon turn left off road, through signed gap in wall. *This marks the southern boundary of the Cotswold Area of Outstanding Natural Beauty, which we have been passing through since entering it near Warmington in Warwickshire (see page 29).* Bear slightly to left of wall-line to right, aiming towards pylon. Start to drop very gently downwards with fine open views ahead. Through small gap in hedge to next field and go through another, larger gap, crossing ill-defined course of Roman road that once ran from Silchester to Bath. Now keep just to right of pylon and head for gap in hedge beneath large oak tree.

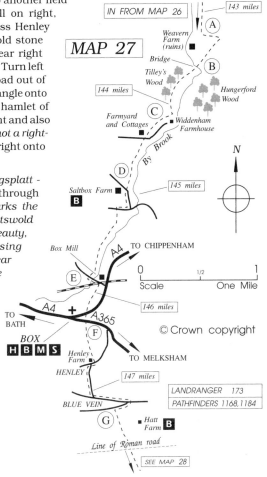

IN FROM MAP 26

143 miles

MAP 27

Weavern Farm (ruins)

A

B

Bridge

Tilley's Wood

144 miles

Hungerford Wood

Farmyard and Cottages

C

Widdenham Farmhouse

By Brook

D

N

145 miles

Saltbox Farm

B

Box Mill

A4

TO CHIPPENHAM

E

0   1/2   1

Scale   One Mile

A4

146 miles

TO BATH

A365

© Crown copyright

BOX

F

H B M S

Henley Farm

TO MELKSHAM

HENLEY

147 miles

BLUE VEIN

LANDRANGER   173

PATHFINDERS 1168,1184

G

Hatt Farm

B

Line of Roman road

SEE MAP 28

61

(A) Through gap beneath oak tree and then over stile to left corner of copse. Keep in same direction, aiming for metal gate in hedge. Through metal gate and head across next field aiming for right-hand end of large building ahead (South Wraxall Manor). Over bridge crossing stream, through metal gate and bear left across paddock, going almost parallel with stream. *Over to left is Manor Farmhouse, in medieval times, a hospice for travellers, complete with chapel.* Over stile in fence and turn sharp right onto narrow road where entrance drive to manor comes in from right. Pass gazebo on right and then gates on right, through which the lovely partly-medieval manor house of South Wraxall can be briefly glimpsed.

(B) Soon turn left over stile (SP - *Public Path*). Down right-hand edge of cricket field and over stile in corner. Turn right through squeeze-stile with house on immediate left and keep straight down driveway. Bear left onto better surfaced road into South Wraxall village with houses on both sides. Turn right at road junction by Willow Cottage and turn left just beyond church, opposite the Longs Arms (SP - *Bradford-on-Avon*). Telephone box on right, opposite inn. *There are several pleasant old stone houses close to the church, which has interesting features including a large squint and several handsome wall monuments.*

(C) Pass village hall on left and, opposite entrance to Church Fields housing estate, turn right through remains of gate. Follow path through gate and go diagonally left across field to Lower Wraxall. Through gate and bear left onto road opposite Mison's Farm. At end of wall, turn right through gate and along path with converted barns on right. Through yet another gate at end of small field and down path with wall on right and hedge on left. Straight, not left, and immediately cross stream onto narrow tarmac lane lined with pleasant old stone houses.

(D) Soon over x-rds onto narrow, but well surfaced road (signed-*No Through Road*). Pass Park Cottage on right. After half-a-mile, bear left at *Bridleway* SP, passing Cherry Orchard farmhouse on right, where tarmac ends. Bend round to right on track which has hedges on both sides. Track now starts to ascend slightly where hedge on left changes to fence. Turn right at junction of tracks with bridleway coming in from left and pass Great Cumberwell Farm, largely to right. Keep on track as it bends to right by high stone wall on right and, ignoring large roadway to left, bear half-left onto moderately surfaced track with power-poles beside it. Pass edge of Cumberwell Park Golf Course on right and, after passing houses on both sides, **cross the busy A363 with care** at offset x-rds (SP - *Ashley*).

(E) Onto minor road (`7.5 tonnes restricted' sign*) and, after about 60 yards, turn left

over stile. Cross field diagonally right to stone stile which is to left of gate (opens into adjacent field) and to right of eight oak trees in hedgeline. Over stile and straight ahead to kissing gate beside field gate. Through kissing gate and go diagonally left across next field to go through another kissing gate to right of line of ash trees.

Town Bridge, Bradford-on-Avon

Continue in same line diagonally across field along well-used path. Spire of Chistchurch, Bradford-on-Avon, visible ahead left. Through kissing gate and across recreation ground (fenced-off children's playground to left).

(F) Through gap in wall to right of metal gate and go slightly left to cross minor road (Ashley Road) at offset 'x-rds' at our entry to Bradford-on-Avon. Go down Huntingdon Street and then cross Winsley Road (B3108). Now go down steep, broad pathway of Conigre Hill. Bear left down steep lane passing Zion Baptist Chapel on right, then bear left ignoring sign *Middle Rank* to right. Turn right onto slightly busier road and almost

South Wraxall Manor

immediately turn left down narrow pathway (opposite house numbered '62' and dated 1695). Turn sharp left and then turn right into Church Street by mill called Dutch Barton. *Plaque on wall states: 'Flemish weavers were brought to this area by clothiers Paul Methuen in 1659 and William Brewer in 1674. Improved techniques re-established the wool trade'.* Pass Abbey Mill on left and turn left over River Avon by footbridge *(but go straight ahead to visit the unique little Saxon church of St Lawrence, on right just beyond).* Good view to left of Abbey Mill when crossing footbridge and then turn left to follow short riverside path to south end of Town Bridge.

(G) Cross St Margaret's Street (A363) with great care to small car park. If traffic busy, use pedestrian crossing up to right.

Ensure that time is spent looking round this beautiful old town, with its steep streets above the river enriched with many splendid examples of 17th- and 18th-century archi-tecture - evidence of its long enduring prosperity as a cloth manufacturing centre. In addition to the little Saxon church, see also the fine parish church opposite and the lovely old Town Bridge with its medieval arches and its stone capped 17th-century lock-up.

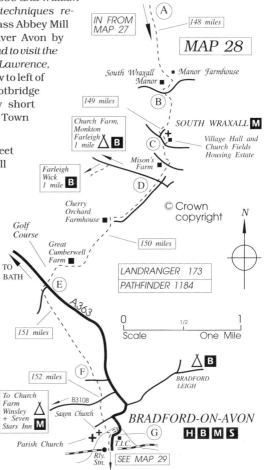

IN FROM MAP 27

A

148 miles

MAP 28

South Wraxall Manor · Manor Farmhouse

149 miles

B

Church Farm, Monkton Farleigh 1 mile △ **B**

SOUTH WRAXALL **M**

C

Village Hall and Church Fields Housing Estate

Mison's Farm

Farleigh Wick 1 mile **B**

D

Cherry Orchard Farmhouse

© Crown copyright

N

Golf Course

Great Cumberwell Farm ■

150 miles

TO BATH

E

A363

LANDRANGER 173

PATHFINDER 1184

151 miles

0   1/2   1
Scale   One Mile

152 miles

F

△ **B**
BRADFORD LEIGH

To Church Farm Winsley + Seven Stars Inn **M**

B3108

Saxon Church

Parish Church

T.I.C.

Rly. Stn.

SEE MAP 29

BRADFORD-ON-AVON

G

H B M S

63

Chapter 6 Bradford-on-Avon - Bruton 32 Miles

(A) Leave Bradford-on-Avon from small car park with adjacent phone boxes, and Museum with Tourist Information Centre, bearing left onto St Margaret's Street (A363) and immediately passing Georgian Lodge Hotel on left. Straight over mini-roundabout leaving A363 and onto B3109 (SP - *Frome*) (road to railway station down to right). Pass attractive Hall's Charity Almshouses on left and over bridge crossing railway line. Keep straight on B3109, but soon turn right, off road between Canal Tavern and Lock Inn Cottage Tearooms, to go down Kennet and Avon Canal towpath. *This is part of the 84-mile-long Kennet and Avon Canal National Waterway Walk, which runs from Reading to Bath.* Pass short path to massive, 14th-century Bradford-on-Avon Tithe Barn on right - well worth a visit. Now on firm, wide towpath with woods up to left beyond tranquil waters of canal. Pass Barton Farm swing-bridge and foot-bridge on left, ignoring footpath waymark to left. Ruined mill on River Avon visible down to right near entry to Avoncliff hamlet. Turn right at aqueduct and then sharp left at Rennie House (B & B), Canal Bookshop and Cross Guns Inn, to go under this handsome 18th-century stone aqueduct - *one of a series constructed by John Rennie, the builder of the Kennet and Avon Canal.* Then bear left up steps onto surfaced road passing Teazel's Coffee Shop and car park on right with Avonvilla (B&B) beyond, also on right.

(B) Go up road out of Avoncliff and soon, where road turns to left, go straight ahead through gap by large wooden gate and onto steep, winding path up through woods. Keep left at fork of tracks by stile down to right and soon bear left onto surfaced road at entry to Upper Westwood. Turn right at road junction by phone box and go straight, not left at next road junction by Chestnut Grove. Pass elegant, early-18th-century house on right and soon, after passing house called *Ashlers* on right, turn left off road (SP - *Lower Westwood*) to go over stone stile and down narrow surfaced path between fences. Now go in same general direction on paths beside roads down through 'The Pastures' housing estate in Westwood.

(C) Bear right at end of estate onto busier road at end of Westwood. *(But turn left if you wish to visit National Trust's fine late 16th-century Westwood Manor - about half-a-mile.)* Bear left at road junction near coach entry to Iford Manor (no entry for walkers here) to go down Iford Hill. Go steeply down hill on road with wall of Iford Manor Gardens on right and soon also on left. Turn left over River Frome opposite Iford Manor on right, crossing bridge complete with figure of Britannia on its parapet. *Try to visit these delightful gardens - the creation of noted landscape architect, Sir Harold Peto, who lived here between 1899 and 1933.*

(D) At 100 yards beyond Iford Bridge, turn left over stile. Go across small field parallel with River Frome. Over stile to left of metal gate, still keeping parallel with river, soon passing attractive weir and into Somerset. Over stile beside metal gate still keeping parallel with river. Farleigh Hungerford's thin church tower just visible on skyline ahead. Start to veer slightly right, away from course of river, following well-used track across field. Through kissing gate beside metal gate and aim across field towards church tower. Over stile beside metal gate and across field

aiming for gate to right of Farleigh Hungerford castle ruins. Over stile beside metal gate and turn sharp left, keeping hedge on immediate left. In bottom corner of small field go over stile and sleeper bridge crossing small stream and bear left by trout farm on right, onto surfaced track. Impressive ruins of Farleigh Hungerford Castle above to right. Bear right, off track onto path below battlements.

Farleigh Hungerford Castle

(E) Turn right up steep, slippery steps. Go straight over roadway at top of slope. *(But turn sharp right through gateway if you wish to visit 14th-century Farleigh Hungerford Castle, with its splendid chapel containing wall paintings, stained glass and the fine tomb of its builder, Sir Thomas Hungerford.)* **Bear slightly right with care, onto busy A366 and face oncoming traffic, being ready to squeeze into verge when vehicles pass.** Just before reaching Hungerford Arms, turn left onto minor road (SP - *Tellisford*) and pass Farleigh Hungerford church on right - *a pleasant little building with a thin tower and a mid-19th-century interior.* Soon pass small conical-roofed, stone water tower on left. Straight, not right at road junction at end of village and down hill overhung with horse-chestnut trees. Pass entrance on right to 19th-century neo-Gothic mansion, Farleigh Castle - now a school.

(F) At next valley bottom, over bridge crossing small stream and almost immediately turn left off road and over stile in hedge (difficult to spot in summer). Go straight across field to left of large ash tree and to right of terrace edge which descends to left. Through gate into woodlands and follow well-used path before emerging into more open field interspersed with trees. Cross field and go through gate with pheasant pens to right. Turn right immediately beyond gate and walk up bank with wood on immediate right. At top of bank, go through hunting gate and follow field boundary with hedge on right, to corner with gateway. Go through gateway and on towards hornbeam hedge by Manor Farmhouse keeping to immediate right of this hedge. Past first gateway, round to left, and through metal gate beyond end of hornbeam hedge before bearing right onto farm drive. At end of farm drive bear right onto road in Tellisford and almost immediately turn sharp left to go down pathway in front of handsome 18th-century Crabb House. Down steep cobbled path with handrail and cross mill stream by ruins of Tellisford Mill on right. Then cross River Frome by attractive arched bridge. Now back into Wiltshire for a short distance.

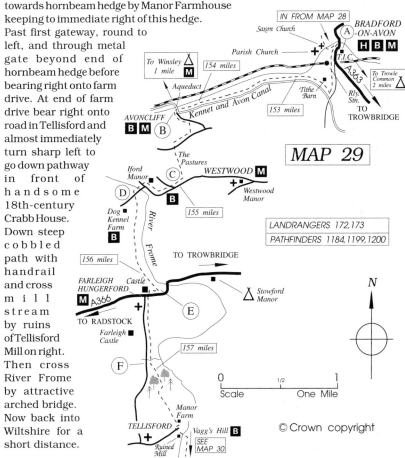

(A) Very soon turn right, leaving surfaced path and over metal stile. Go across field with River Frome some distance to right, soon passing weir on right. *World War II pillbox on right - probably part of a defensive line along the east bank of the Frome.* Over wooden stile beyond pillbox, with tranquil waters of River Frome also just to right. Keep to left-hand edge of field with wood on immediate left and then bear slightly to left to go through metal gate to left of small farm outbuildings onto surfaced road. Pass Langham Farmhouse on right - *delicious honey usually available here.* Along pleasant shady road with River Frome down to right. Pass anglers' car park on right, and now cross back into Somerset. Keep on track across more open field. Rode Church, with two unusual miniature 'spires' at its west end, soon visible ahead *(this is closed due to dangerous masonry).* Over stile beside cattle-grid at entry to Rode and pass handsome 18th-century house on right.

(B) Cross busier road (SP - *Rode*), soon bend round to right by small green with war memorial to left and pass bus shelter and phone box on left. Keep straight up High Street passing Cross Keys Inn on left and old school building on left. Straight, not right, at end of village by Merfield Lodge and almost immediately turn left, up Crooked Lane. At T-junction at end of lane go straight ahead onto narrow trackway overhung with trees. Through gap in hedge and into field, now keeping in same direction with hedge line on immediate left.

(C) Over stile at end of field and climb embankment to cross busy A36 **with very great care**. Go down embankment, then left along base of embankment, before going over stile on right and then keeping to left-hand edge of field. Over rudimentary stile into next field and keep on same line aiming for next stile. Over stile and go across recreation ground, veering right to avoid most of games pitches. Go through metal gate to left of club buildings, cross road *(but turn left if you wish to go to Little Chef and/or Travel Lodge)* and bear left at entry to village of Beckington, with its wealth of pleasant old stone buildings. Keep on road into Beckington and bear right in centre of village keeping on wider road (Frome Road) by Woolpack Inn on left (SP - *Oldford*). *Two shops up to left, while a little further on, just beyond the Woolpack Inn, a second road leads up left to the church with its outstandingly beautiful Norman tower and its interesting interior.*

(D) Pass bus stop on left and at far end of village, opposite layby on left, turn right up Stubbs Lane (track) by small conical roofed gazebo. Go down surfaced farm road passing sign - *The Staplemead Herd of British Friesians.* Pass modern barn on left and almost immediately fork left over rudimentary stile in wire fence. Go along slight terrace across field aiming for stile beside metal gate. Part of Orchardleigh Golf Course visible ahead beyond valley. Over stile beside metal gate with Dairy House Farm well down to right. Head diagonally right across field aiming for stile

beside metal gate. Over this stile and keep in same direction across field aiming for metal gate. Through gateway to left of water trough and head across field aiming for stile beneath ash tree. *World War II pillbox over to right, on banks of River Frome - similar to the one just beyond Tellisford.* Creamery chimney visible down valley to left.

Beckington Church

(E) Over stile and metal footbridge across River Frome and go diagonally right to cross stile at

right-hand corner of narrow field. Cross road and over stile. Up small bank and turn right to follow to immediate left of trees and hedge lining small tributary stream, with edge of Orchardleigh Golf Course to left. Cross surfaced drive with bridge to immediate right, with views up drive beyond to attractive early 19th-century 'Gothick' gatehouse, known as Gloucester Lodge. Pass waymark on post and at second waymark on post turn right

Cottages at Lullington

onto track. Through small wooden gate beside large one and bear left onto surfaced road with cottage up to right. Bear left onto road near phone box at entry to village of Lullington and almost immediately left by attractive green complete with old hand-pump. *The church is over to the right, beyond the green, and is one of the more interesting ones to be found on our route. See especially the north doorway, the font and the tower arches - all beautiful specimens of Norman craftsmanship.* Pass Yew Tree Cottage on left and Gloucester Farm on left.

(F) Where road bends sharply right, go straight ahead through gate, keeping hedge on left. Follow farm track to go through gate and continue across field to left of oak trees. Bear very slightly left to stile in wire fence. Over stile and, with eyes open for possibly hazardous golf balls, keep in same direction across golf course in Orchardleigh Park, heading towards right-hand end of old stable building. Neo-Elizabethan Orchardleigh House now visible over to left. Arrive at post on surfaced road with a number of waymarks and bear half right onto this road. Ignore sign on left to church. After 500 yards go through gate at exit from Golf Club.

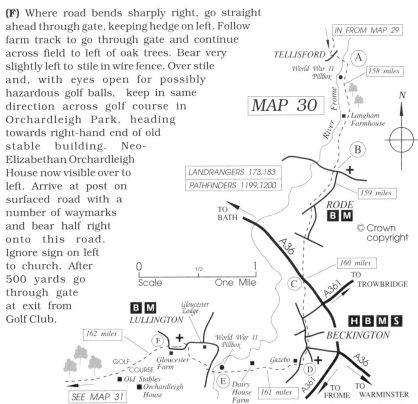

67

(A) Beyond gate at end of Orchardleigh Golf Club, bear half-right, off roadway, and first keeping edge of Orchardleigh Wood on immediate right, go straight ahead (almost due east) in open parkland towards wooded area. Take great care to keep on right course in this area - we route planners lost ourselves here - twice! Veer slightly right, first over rough grass with bushes, and then go between single oak on left and two poplars just to right. Soon enter more dense woodland joining track coming in from left by small waymark. Continue in same direction on track, going slightly downhill and passing small sign on right stating *Conservation Area*. Over 'crossroads' of tracks with pheasant pens and other small buildings well over to left and keep on track in same direction through woods. After about 250 yards go straight ahead on well defined, grassy path, where track bends sharply to right and grassy ride comes in from left.

(B) Leave wood through gap to right of broken stile and over small sleeper bridge into field with woodlands still on right-hand side. Head straight down ever-narrowing field, initially with wood on right and then only hedge with trees. Go through gateway, bear slightly left and immediately through gap beyond, at meeting of four fields, ignoring grassy track up to left. Head straight across field aiming just to left of Buckland Dinham church, visible on hill ahead, and just to left of solitary ash tree. Pass tree and go over metal-railed footbridge near left-hand corner of field. Over small field, veering slightly left and over wooden footbridge. Go diagonally up large, steeply sloping field aiming for clump of pine trees. Over stile to left of metal gate at top of field, at entry to attractive stone and thatch, hill-top village of Buckland Dinham and go beside wall, up lane leading to church.

(C) Pass lych gate on right, *noting church with its Norman south doorway within a splendidly vaulted porch and its fine Perpendicular tower, and also the little village lockup opposite the church.* Turn left down small road from church passing phone box on right and turn right onto busy A362 opposite village hall. After about 100 yards, turn left just beyond bus shelter on right, go up small tarmac lane between houses *(but go straight for Bell Inn)*. Go onto narrow path, first tarmac and then grassy, to go over stile and then bear slightly left in narrow field keeping wall and then hedge on immediate left. Distant view ahead of Alfred's Tower (see pages 72-73), on wooded northerly confines of Stourhead Estate. Over stone stile and go down field keeping hedge on immediate left. Over stile to left, down across field to go over stile and then cross minor road.

(D) Immediately over stone stile beyond road. Continue in same direction across field aiming just to left of low, white house beneath trees some distance ahead. At end of field, over stile and sleeper bridge and veer diagonally half-right (almost due

south) aiming to left of two ash trees on right-hand edge of large field. Through gate, over track and bear right through gap to follow slight incline up right-hand edge of narrow field. Over stile in hedge beneath small oak tree and turn left to go down minor road. Go along road for about 500 yards, then under railway bridge and go another 500 yards before bearing right onto busier road at entry to quiet village of Great Elm, poised above wooded valley of Mells Stream.

(E) After 200 yards, where road bends round to right, bear left by metal bollard, and down steep little tree-shaded path with walls on either side *(but go straight ahead if you wish to visit early Norman church - on right after 150 yards)*. At bottom of path turn sharp left onto minor road, then bear right over bridge crossing Mells Stream, here dammed up to

Duckpond at Great Elm

form attractive duckpond. Ignore footpath signs to right *(unless you wish to divert to Mells - fine church and hospitable Talbot Inn - under two miles)* and keep on road as it bends left up through woodland. Halfway up hill turn right onto track in wood *joining the East Mendip Way - a 19-mile County Path between Frome and Wells.* Bear right at top of track and follow well-used path within wood with its fenced edge close to left. Happily there is little sign of the great quarries ahead right, but railway line and Mells Stream are just visible down to right in places. Path starts to ascend a little before going between two massive stones at Murder Combe *(we could find no clues as to the origin of this place-name).*

(F) Turn left with care onto busy road and almost immediately turn right to go over stile onto track. Along track bending slightly to right, with hedge on immediate left, trees to right, the latter soon finishing as track peters out. Through pasture field still keeping hedge on left. Whatley church spire soon visible ahead. *Now leaving the course of the East Mendip Way which turns right in this area.* Keep on same line with fence on left and over stile below ash tree at far left-hand end of field. Now go along right-hand edge of next field with hazel hedge on immediate right. Over stile to left of water trough and keep along next field with hedge on immediate right, still aiming for Whatley church spire. Turn right, over stile in corner of field and turn immediately left to go over stile in cross hedge a few yards out from left. Now veer left to cross small portion of field diagonally and over stile in left-hand hedge. Up narrow path into fragmented village of Whatley with hedge on left and fence on right and pass bungalow called *Fortywinks* on right. Down tarmac driveway for a few yards before bearing left onto parallel path. Soon re-join driveway, bearing right where track comes in from left.

(G) Now bear left with care onto minor road by entry to Whatley Vineyard. **Walk along road with care** for about 100 yards and turn right onto track beside Sun Inn. Soon over stile into field on right and bear left, diagonally across field, aiming for Alfred's Tower on skyline and kissing gate. Through gate, leaving right-of-way, and turn left (south-east) onto permissive path alongside hedge (kindly allowed by Mr John Norris). Climb railed fence and cross road to go down good track (also permissive - kindly allowed by Mr Michael Toop).

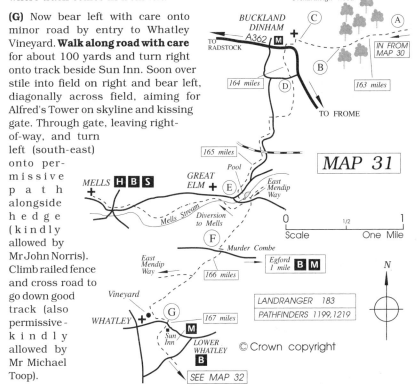

69

(A) After about 150 yards cross Nunney Brook in Nunney Combe re-joining right-of-way and immediately turn right onto path with Nunney Brook now on right. Pass small plantation of poplars on right. Pass horse jumps in field and sewage works over to right. Keep straight across meadow (ignoring metal gate and stile to right). Over stile and into park-like garden of Combe Farm, farmhouse visible up to right beyond stream. Walk up tree-lined drive and through gate. Onto road, passing house with high wall on right and drop down into delightful village of Nunney.

(B) Turn right onto Frome Road by Rose Cottage and go through village, with restored market cross, duckpond and castle on right and church on left. *With its moat and elegant round towers, Nunney has a real flavour of France - everyone's dream of a perfect medieval castle. It's builder, Sir John de la Mare, lies in the church opposite, which also has fine monuments in its north aisle chapel and a Norman font with a Jacobean conical font cover.* Pass 'The George at Nunney' Hotel on left and Market Place with village shop on right. Go straight, not right by phone box (SP - *Witham Friary*). Head up hill out of village and fork left by Nunney First School walking with care on busier road.

(C) In Nunney Catch hamlet go straight ahead to immediate left of Theobald Arms, leaving road and down cul-de-sac to go under subway beneath very busy A361 *(but bear right keeping on road by Theobald Arms for Little Chef, by roundabout a short distance ahead)*. Beyond subway bear left onto still busy minor road. Walk down road **with great care** going straight, not left near Pyle Farm, where entry to Trudoxhill is signed. Pass chapel on left and keep straight through Trudoxhill until forking left (SP - *Marston*) by White Hart Inn, with the little Ash Vine Brewery at its rear. Leave village on road ignoring footpath signs to left.

(D) Where road bends sharply to left (about 200 yards beyond village) go straight ahead through metal gate and continue in same direction, across right-hand side of field, aiming for Nutty Coppice Farmhouse. Through metal gate in cross-hedge and over next field aiming for stile in line with farmhouse. Over stile in cross-hedge and, veering slightly right, aim for right-hand end of farm buildings. Through gap in corner of field and up track with farm buildings to left. Soon over stile, up short farm drive to join road and fork left (SP - *Gare Hill*).

(E) Almost immediately turn right off road and through bushes to go to right of main bus garage at back of Lawns Farm. Over stile below large oak tree and go down long, narrow field with oak trees on both sides. Turn left through gateway in far left-hand corner of field and immediately turn right to follow as close as possible to right hand hedge (partially obscured by bushes). Over double stile in far right-hand corner of

field and keep straight across next field. Alfred's Tower (see pages 72-73) now visible at southern end of long, wooded ridge ahead. Soon aim for large metal gate to left of water trough. Through this gate and keep down field with hedge to immediate left, passing under pylon line. Through wooden gate and down fenced farm track. Turn left onto road and soon over Witham Bridge crossing infant River Frome. *(Note attractive fishing lakes back right. These were once used by the monks of Witham Priory - see below.)* Turn right, leaving road opposite large concrete silage store of Witham Hall Farm, and through large metal gate. Up field keeping to immediate right of hedge.

The fields to left were once covered by buildings of a large Carthusian Priory, known latterly as Witham Friary. The remaining earthworks are not very revealing but a large priory was established here as part of Henry II's penance for the murder of Archbishop Thomas Becket in 1170. This was the first and mother house of the Carthusians in England, the Carthusians being the strictest and most austere of all religious orders. It was dissolved in 1539 and its buildings were acquired by Ralph Hopton, who converted them into a residence. This was purchased by Sir William Wyndham in the 18th century and he built a fine Palladian mansion here, Witham House, to the design of William Talman. The house then passed into the hands of Alderman Beckford who started to build a new house on a small hill nearby, but he died long before it was completed and the energies of his eccentric son, the noted William Beckford, were soon concentrated on the building of the equally ill-fated Fonthill. Thus the mansion at Witham fell into disrepair and now nothing remains apart from the long, straight green roads which we shall use shortly - they were once part of the grandiose approach drive to the mansion.

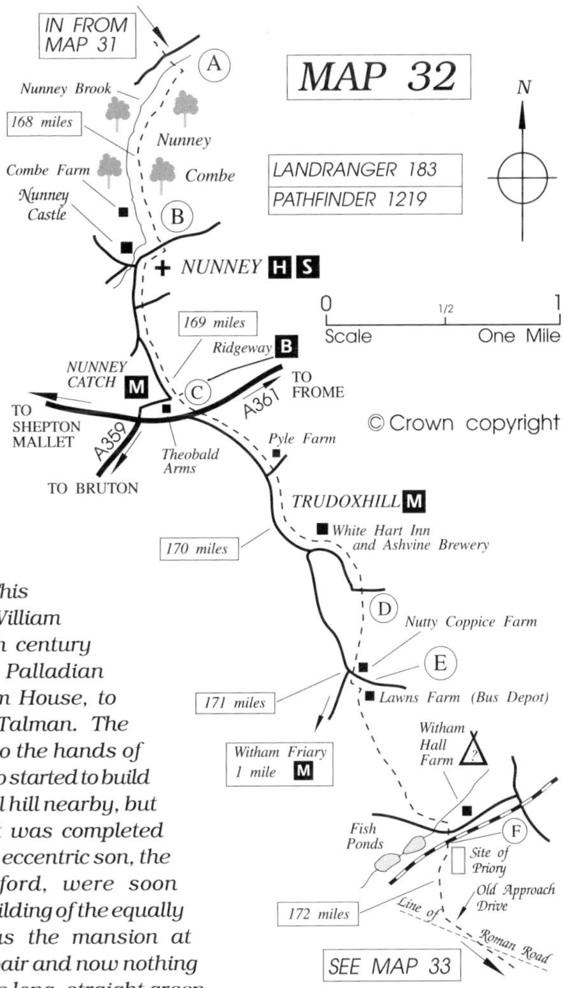

IN FROM MAP 31

A

MAP 32

N

Nunney Brook

168 miles

Nunney

Combe Farm

Combe

Nunney Castle

B

LANDRANGER 183
PATHFINDER 1219

+ NUNNEY H S

0   1/2   1
Scale   One Mile

169 miles

Ridgeway B

NUNNEY CATCH M

C

TO FROME

TO SHEPTON MALLET

A359

A361

Theobald Arms

Pyle Farm

© Crown copyright

TO BRUTON

TRUDOXHILL M

White Hart Inn and Ashvine Brewery

170 miles

D

Nutty Coppice Farm

E

171 miles

Lawns Farm (Bus Depot)

Witham Hall Farm

Witham Friary 1 mile M

Fish Ponds

F

Site of Priory

Old Approach Drive

172 miles

Line of

Roman Road

SEE MAP 33

(F) Over stile and **cross very busy railway line with great care** - 'Stop, Look, Listen' as the notice states. The trains may not go as fast as their French or Japanese counterparts, but they are still extremely dangerous. Over second stile and up field in same direction, keeping to immediate right of hedge. Gare Hill Church visible in gap in trees on ridge ahead left. Through metal gate and go across field veering only slightly left of previous line and once over brow, aim for hunting rails in hedge. Climb carefully over hunting rails and go down long, wide green-road with hedges on both sides *(this was part of the old approach drive to long-vanished Witham House - see above)*. Just before reaching Walk Farm, cross course of Roman road that once ran from Salisbury to the lead mines near Charterhouse in the Mendips, although there are no obvious signs here.

(A) Through metal gate and pass to immediate left of Walk Farm. Initially keep in same direction, crossing two farm tracks by farmhouse on right. Through metal gate and bear right beyond last buildings over to right, keeping on wide farm track between hedges - a continuation of green-road. Now heading straight towards wooded ridge marking border with Wiltshire. Through metal gate at end of track, but green-road still continues with hedges on both sides.

(B) Through metal gate where track appears to end, although hedge continues on right with wood beyond on right known as Pound Copse and signs of old hedge-line continue to left and also signs of surfacing amongst grass. Through gate and onto surfaced track again, with hedge to right and fence to left. Now starting to climb gently and through two metal gates where track comes in from left. Splendid views opening up behind (northwards). Pass farm buildings on right, through metal gate and pass drive to Witham Park Farm's farmhouse on right.

(C) At entry to Witham Park woodlands, turn right onto permissive forest track. Cross footpath keeping on track and over stile to right of wooden gate. Turn right onto road and where it bends to right, go straight ahead into West End Wood, through wooden gate onto permissive forest track and ignore track up hill to left with *No Through Road* sign. Continue on track passing brick building in trees on right and bear right up slight rise with good views to right where trees are thin. Bear right and track becomes worn and boggy in parts.

(D) Turn right onto road and shortly after passing Druly Hill Farm on right, turn left off road at entry to Forestry Commission's King's Wood Warren woodlands, by going through small gate. (Notice states: *Keep dogs on lead please*). Go down well surfaced forest road, very soon ignoring small pathway up to left. Keep straight at Y-junction, going upwards (rather than right, downwards). Pleasant track at start with woods to right and bracken covered slopes up to left with trees beyond (but character of woods will change many times before we arrive in vicinity of Alfred's Tower - still some way ahead). Keep on track where it bends to right, thus going onto a short permissive section and ignoring path up to left. Woodlands now on both sides. At next junction of tracks, keep straight, going upwards, not right. Pass large wooden foresters' hut on left. Fork left off main track and go around security barrier to join narrower track (Notice on right of main track states *No unauthorised vehicles)*. Continue with wire fence now to right and ignore small stile on right with waymark. Forest ends on right, with field beyond line of beech trees on right of path. Go around security barrier onto road.

(E) Go straight over this road with care, joining the Leland Trail (see below) (SP - *Aaron's Hill). But turn left and go up wooded hill on road for 250 yards if you wish to visit the National Trust's Alfred's Tower, on right of road at top of hill. This massive*

160ft-high, triangular tower in mellow brick was built in 1772 to mark the place where King Alfred probably set up his standard in the year 878 at the start of his eventually successful campaign to repel the Danes. It contains a staircase and can be climbed when open.

Alfred's Tower also marks the start of the Leland Trail, a 28-mile walking route ending at Ham Hill, near Montacute. This was developed by South Somerset District Council and we shall follow it for

Stourhead

about 17 miles, only leaving it at South Cadbury. It is named after the 16th-century antiquary, John Leland, who travelled through Somerset at some time between 1535 and 1543 while compiling his great 'Itinerary'.

It is also possible to walk beyond Alfred's Tower down to the National Trust's elegant Palladian mansion of Stourhead and its magnificently landscaped gardens - a distance of just over two miles. The path drops down through pleasant woodlands, joining a minor road into Stourton village by Stourhead's Rock Arch.

(E) If you have diverted from main route, now return to beginning of footpath at bottom of hill (SP - *Aaron's Hill*) and turning left into more woods. Go straight, not left at Y-junction of paths. Go straight, not right, at next Y-junction of paths and start to drop into valley. Bear left joining footpath with waymarks pointing both ways and almost immediately bear left again at T-junction of tracks. Now climb up track as it bends to right and, at top of slope, keep straight where another track comes in from left.

(F) Turn right at cross-roads of tracks and then bear right onto surfaced road. Pass through security barrier and follow road as it bends to left and right. Then where road bends again to left, fork right up track (SP - *Redlynch 3 miles*). Go uphill on sunken trackway in Blackslough Wood and then start to descend slightly. Fork right at junction of tracks and footpaths and continue down hill. Straight, not right, keeping on main track soon passing rhododendrons on right before forking left. Over stile beside wooden gate and pass field to right, with woods still to left. Continue in same direction on track across field as woods end on left, and soon go straight, not right, to pass along left-hand side of small wood.

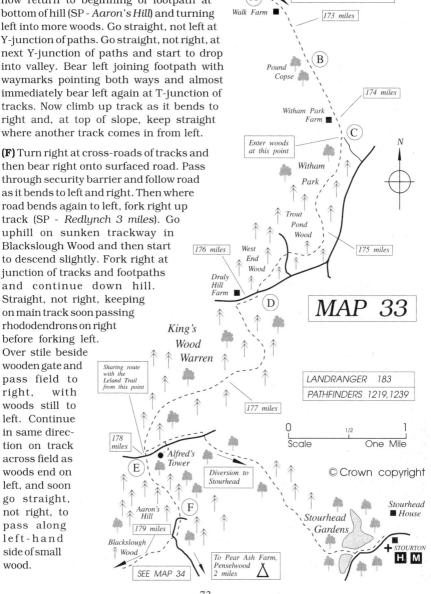

IN FROM MAP 32

Walk Farm

173 miles

A

Pound Copse

B

174 miles

Witham Park Farm

C

N

Enter woods at this point

Witham

Park

Trout Pond Wood

West End Wood

176 miles

175 miles

Druly Hill Farm

D

MAP 33

King's Wood Warren

LANDRANGER 183
PATHFINDERS 1219, 1239

Sharing route with the Leland Trail from this point

177 miles

0   1/2   1
Scale   One Mile

178 miles

Alfred's Tower

E

Diversion to Stourhead

© Crown copyright

Aaron's Hill

F

Stourhead House

Stourhead Gardens

179 miles

Blackslough Wood

SEE MAP 34

To Pear Ash Farm, Penselwood 2 miles

STOURTON
H M

73

(A) At far corner of wood, bear half-right across field aiming for stile. Over pair of stiles and cross next field. *From here we shall go in an almost straight line for over two miles, following the course of a supposed 'old coach road' until reaching Redlynch. However, this was probably a drive to the mansion of Redlynch, connecting it with the coach road from London and also perhaps with Stourhead. Sometimes known as the Hard Way, it may also have been used by drovers taking cattle to the London markets.* Pass wood on immediate right (this is the remains of Stavordale Wood which appears to have been largely cleared on the left (south) side). Path soon becomes a track again. Over stile beside gate; wood still on right, hedge on left. Through metal gate and continue on fenced track. Good views of Alfred's Tower back right. At T-junction of tracks go straight across and over stile on other side. Cross field in same direction and over stile beside metal gate. Go straight up field and over stile. Keep in same direction on farm track and over stile beside metal gate. Keep straight through Coachroad Farm's farmyard, with barn to left and farmhouse to right.

(B) Over stile at end of yard, cross road and over second stile (SP - *Redlynch*). Keep in same direction across field, over stile beside metal gate and across small field on track. Good views northwards over low rolling country and back, eastwards, to Alfred's Tower. Over stile beside metal gate and continue on track across next field. Foundations of 'Old Coach Road' visible in grass here. Pass small wood known as Walk Copse on left, over stile beside metal gate and continue straight across next field following slightly raised course of old road. Over stile beside metal gate and pass substantial farm with large garden and pool beyond fence to right.

(C) Follow to immediate left of wire fence and up slight incline across large field. At end of large field, over stile just beyond thatched Moor Wood Cottage on left. Go between wire fences, follow round to left of small outbuilding and head diagonally left to go over stile beside wooden gate. Resume original line of walk by going up track with fence to right and attractive open woodlands known as Moor Wood to left. Over stile beside metal gate at end of wood on left. Continue across field up avenue of young oaks.

(D) Over pair of stiles and turn right with care onto busy B3081 opposite gateway to Redlynch Park - our first significant change of direction for over two miles. *Redlynch, now a ruin following a disastrous fire, was the home of that great 18th-century politician, Charles James Fox.* Keep well into side of road and soon turn left at cross-roads (SP - *Shepton Montague*). Pass Redlynch Farm on right and beyond houses on right turn right, off road, opposite handsome little 18th-century Redlynch Church and over stile beside metal gate (SP - *Bruton*). Head up right-hand side of field with hedge on immediate right and over pair of stiles and sleeper bridge in top right-hand corner of field. Initially keep to immediate left of hedge, but when this

Packhorse Bridge at Bruton

74

turns right, go straight across field keeping just to right of small mound and soon aiming for stile. Over stile beside metal gate, keep down field in same direction with hedge to immediate right. Glastonbury Tor visible well over to left.

(E) Pass hedge with Droppinglane Farm's buildings beyond to right and over stile to right of bushes. Bear left, maintaining same line as previously, to go over stile beside metal gate. Now veer slightly left to go across field keeping just to left of hedge-line. Over stile about three yards to right of metal gate, keep down field to immediate left of hedge. Almost at bottom of field, turn right through hedge on right, crossing pair of stiles and sleeper bridge. Go down field keeping to right of hedge and after 150 yards, where hedge veers to left, go diagonally across field to stile at bottom of field. Bruton Dovecot visible well ahead left.

(F) Over this stile beside metal gate, turn right onto minor road and immediately turn left with care onto B3081 (not signed). After about 40 yards fork left off B3081 onto minor road by metal bench on left *(7.5 tonne Restriction Sign)*. Take care on narrow, but quite busy road with virtually no verges. *Pass field entry to National Trust's impressive 16th-century dovecot, above to right. This once belonged to Bruton Abbey.* At entry to Bruton, turn right into Godminster Lane, over bridge crossing railway line and bear right onto wider road (Silver Street) (no sign). Go along Silver Street passing buildings of King's School on both sides, including precinct wall of Bruton's once great abbey on right. At this point the intrepid can cross the little River Brue by turning left and using stepping stones, although the more cautious walker will turn left just beyond to go over attractive packhorse bridge.

But go straight ahead if first wishing to visit church - on right just beyond. This is a splendid, largely Perpendicular style building, with an early 14th-century crypt, a tall graceful tower, and an unusually elegant Roccoco chancel. The latter comes as a shock when a medieval interior is expected, but it is very impressive. See also the fine early Renaissance tomb in a recess in the chancel, with the reclining figure of Sir Maurice Berkeley, who died in 1506 and who was Standard Bearer to Henry VII, Henry VIII, Edward VI and Queen Elizabeth). Bruton is a delightful little town, as yet unspoilt by tourism. Its narrow High Street is lined with small shops and inns and, near its western end, the attractive Sexey's Hospital - almshouses complete with chapel and hall. Douglas Macmillan, the founder of the organisation now known as Cancer Relief Macmillan Fund, went to Sexey's School, the buildings of which lie to the south-west of the town. For more details about Douglas Macmillan, see page 6.

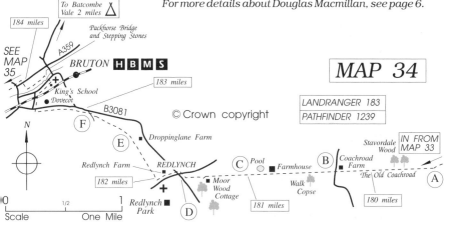

MAP 34

LANDRANGER 183
PATHFINDER 1239

© Crown copyright

Chapter 7   Bruton - Abbotsbury   51 Miles

(A) To resume our walk - turn left beyond Bruton's packhorse bridge (or nearby stepping stones) into Lower Backway. Go straight along Lower Backway *(but turn right up one of several narrow passages (known locally as 'bartons') if you wish to visit shops or inns in the High Street)*. Turn right at end of Lower Backway and soon turn left by Town Mill House into far end of High Street to pass phone box on left.

(B) At end of High Street, go straight over road with care at Y-junction and, beside right-hand end of garage, up narrow Trendle Lane. Where tarmac driveway bends to left, go straight on up sunken trackway overhung with trees. By farm gates on right, follow track as it veers slightly right and becomes wider farm track. At about highest point, hedge to left eventually ends, but track continues with hedge on right.

(C) Turn right to cross stile and go immediately left to follow close to right of hedge. *Good view ahead right includes Glastonbury Tor and, on a clear day, the distant line of the Quantocks.* Where this short hedge turns to left, veer half-right to go over field to stile in cross-fence. Keep in same direction down bank aiming for stile. Over offset pair of stiles crossing concrete farm road and go straight across field aiming well to right of buildings, one of which is on a mound. *These buildings include mellow-stoned Wyke Champflower Manor, to which is attached a small 17th-century church. Built in the 17th century, it has a delightfully unspoilt interior complete with an elaborate stone pulpit, a painted tympanum dividing the ceilings of the chancel and nave and also Jacobean box pews, each with its own hat peg.*

(D) Turn left onto road, soon passing driveway to Wyke Champflower's manor and church on left *(do try to visit this)* and then over bridge crossing remains of railway (the old Somerset and Dorset line). Immediately turn left at road junction keeping on road. Under railway bridge just beyond modern house on left and continue along road, ignoring waymark up to left where our road bends sharply down to right. Down this narrow sunken road to go under yet another railway bridge.

(E) Over bridge crossing stream and turn right at T-junction in Cole hamlet by Manor House on right. *Douglas Macmillan must have walked through this hamlet many hundreds of times on his daily journey between his home at Castle Cary and his school at Bruton - a distance of almost three miles each way.* Keep on road passing Manor Farm and Cole Farmhouse, both on right. Where road bears left beyond Cole Farm, fork right and over stile (SP - *Ridge Hill*). Go diagonally left, down to far corner of field, then bear right into corner and cross brook on concrete bridge. Go up through orchard to waymark, turn left and walk along upper edge of orchard with hedge on right. Over stile at top corner of orchard and up field with hedge to immediate right. Pleasant views across orchards in valley to left. Alfred's Tower still visible beyond Bruton, with the latter's church tower and dovecote well in view. At top of Ridge Hill bear left following fence line to immediate right. Bear right still

following fence line to right, with small valley coming up from left. Turn right going over stile in far right-hand corner and across small field with hedge on left.

(F) Over stile, down sunken path and turn left onto sunken roadway. Ignore bridleway sign to left, and soon turn right (SP - *Ansford*) up sunken trackway, known as Solomon's Lane. This narrows in part to become pathway pleasantly overhung with bushes. Track starts to drop by stout wooden fence on right and outskirts of Higher Ansford just visible ahead. Straight, not right, at junction of sunken tracks and then turn right onto road in Higher Ansford by Ansford Farmhouse. Soon turn left at road junction by elegantly porched 18th-century Ansford House and down Ansford Road into Castle Cary. Pass turning to car park on right and turn right at T-junction by Highfield House into Castle Cary's High Street. Pass Old Bakehouse Restaurant on right, Market Hall on right. Phone box by Market Hall.

Castle Cary is a delightful little market town situated below the earthworks of its early 12th-century castle, with colourful shops, hotels and inns - all full of character. The Victorian Market Hall is now partly a museum and Tourist Information Centre. Just behind it is the handsome 18th-century stone Post Office and the Round House or Pepper Pot, a stout little circular lock-up built in 1779. The slender-spired church lies some way beyond our route and was largely re-built in the same year as the Market Hall - 1855. Douglas Macmillan was born in Castle Cary in 1884 and grew up here (see also page 6).

(G) Turn left immediately beyond George Hotel and go up Paddock Drain, a narrow, ascending passage (note vine on wall of George Hotel to left). Over stile near Castle Cary Castle explanatory board and turn left following left-hand of two waymarks. Go straight up hill with fence line to immediate left. *Soon pass earthworks of castle to immediate right but these are better viewed from above, a few minutes walk along path. Glastonbury Tor soon visible, back over the town.* Over stile in cross-fence and continue in same line before bearing right to aim for post and bench near top of Lodge Hill. *This bench makes a fine viewing (and resting!) point, with Mendips, Glastonbury Tor, Somerset Levels and Quantocks - all visible on a clear day.* Continue in same direction from bench, with hedge over to left and go over stile beside metal gate. Keep in same direction and then, just beyond concrete water trough, ignore waymarked stile ahead and turn left over stile in fence. Now head southwards with fence to immediate right, soon passing storage tank and low farm building on right.

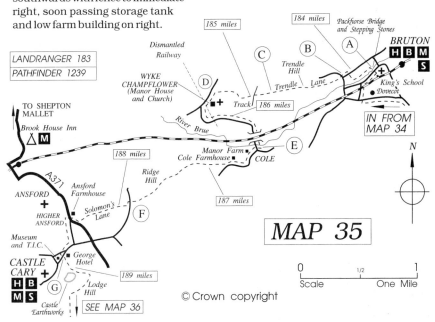

(A) Cross farm track, over stile beyond it and initially go along field with fence to right. Soon turn right over stile just beyond metal gate and veer to right of previous line to go to right-hand end of projecting cross-wall with hedge. Once round this corner follow down field to immediate right of field edge. Just before cross-fence ahead turn left over stile and go up left-hand edge of field. Bear right at end of field to go in front of electricity sub-station and turn left onto A359. Walk down A359 **with great care** and soon, first ignoring tempting track down to right, turn right through hunting gate just beyond it (SP - Woolston). Down field with large hedge and overgrown trackway to immediate right and through metal gate. Keep down next field with hedge on right and decaying metal windpump on left.

(B) Through hunting gate at end of field, joining track known as Hick's Lane, and continue in same direction. Lane eventually becomes sunken with overhanging trees and its banks perforated by fox earths. At end of Hicks Lane go straight ahead onto road.

(C) After 200 yards turn right over stile beside large metal gates (SP - *Brookhampton*). Straight across field, first going just to left of concrete water trough and then past single oak tree to stile well beyond. Over stile in cross-hedge and go diagonally left across slightly smaller field to far left-hand corner, keeping just to left of another single oak tree. Small stream now over to left - this is River Cam, which flows into River Yeo just to east of Yeovilton. Over sleeper bridge crossing small tributary brook and over stile just beyond. Over even smaller field heading for corner in bushes, with stream still to immediate left. Over double-stile and across small orchard still keeping stream to immediate left. Over double-stile with sleeper bridge between and across next field with stream and hedge to left. Just before corner of field, turn left to cross stile and concrete and steel bridge over stream. Immediately turn right with River Cam and line of alder trees now on right. At end of field, turn right before reaching house and go back over River Cam on wide, wooden bridge.

(D) Cross end of small field and over stile to turn left onto road, known here as

Sandbrook Lane. Pass millhouse with re-located water wheel and extensive garden on left. Go straight, not left, at road junction by Bridge Cottage on left. After about 300 yards fork left over stile off Sandbrook Lane (SP - *Brookhampton*). Now continue in same direction along narrow field, keeping parallel with roadside hedge to right and stream to left. Turn left over stile by metal gate re-joining Sandbrook Lane and cross bridge over River Cam.

(E) Soon, after road bends to right, turn left, up steps and over stile. Go diagonally across field and over stile in far left-hand corner. Along field keeping hedge on immediate left, over stile and continue along left-hand edge of North Cadbury School playing-field. Over stile and keep straight along path with hedges on both sides. Fork right (ignoring SP - Woolston) *(Now leaving originally planned Leland Trail, although, like us, many walkers now follow road to avoid dangerous crossing of A303).* Over bridge and along often muddy

The Catash Inn, North Cadbury

path. Soon onto surfaced driveway and bear left onto road at entry to quiet village of North Cadbury. Turn right at end of Cutty Lane into High Street and then turn left just beyond Catash Inn. Pass bus shelter and phone box on right.

(F) Straight, not left at end of village, keeping on road (SP - *South Cadbury*). After about 100 yards, pass steps on left up to path leading to North Cadbury Church. *This fine church stands beside the equally impressive Elizabethan mansion of North Cadbury Court, and is well worth a short diversion. Its beautiful chancel was built to accomodate a college of priests, although for some reason this institution was never established. Beneath the tower is a handsome monument to Lady Botreaux, the builder of most of the church and to her husband, William. The magnificent roof is supported on angel corbel figures and light floods in through much clear glass - always a welcome change after the dark* Victorian stained glass encountered in so many churches. There are also old flagged floors, a number of 16th-century carved bench ends and, in the vestry, a medieval alphabet for the instruction of children. Now head southwards down road with great care. *Good views of wooded slopes of Cadbury Castle (hill fort) ahead.* Pass Chapel Cross Cottage on left and straight, not right by small thatched chapel attached to cottage, over to right. *This was noted by Tudor antiquary, John Leland who wrote, 'I turnid flat west by a little chapelle'.*

(G) However, our own route continues southwards (SP-*South Cadbury*), going over bridge crossing busy A303 and then straight, not right (SP - *South Cadbury*). Keep on road into South Cadbury, *a small village dominated by the impressive earthworks of Cadbury Castle, which rises just beyond.* Keep straight through South Cadbury, passing phone box on right. Go over x-rds by Red Lion Inn (SP - *Corton Denham*), finally leaving the Leland Trail. Pass church on right. *This has a late 14th-century tower but most of the rest was rebuilt in Victorian times.*

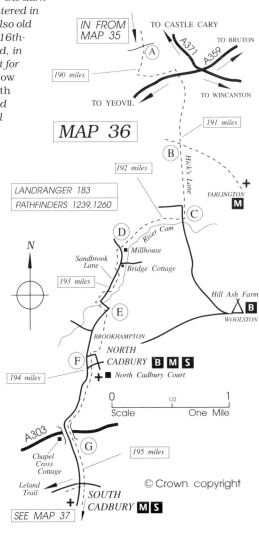

(A) Soon go straight, not right, keeping on road. *But turn right if you wish to climb up steep track to Cadbury Castle earthworks, from which there are outstanding views - a strongly recommended diversion - even for the weariest of walkers!). Cadbury Castle is a massive, 18-acre Iron Age hill fort at the meeting point of a number of ancient trackways. It is guarded by four massive banks and ditches and is likely to have been a key fortress during the years following the withdrawal of the Roman legions - the Celtic twilight. Referring to this fort, our friend the antiquary, John Leland states that, 'The people can telle nothing ther but that they have hard say that Arture much resorted to Camalat', and this place may at least have partly inspired the legends of Arthur and his Knights of the Round Table. However, extensive excavations in the 1960s sadly failed to solve this, its greatest mystery. So, having sampled the outstanding views from its ramparts, let us cease to dream ---* and instead, drop down to the road and head southwards once again soon passing small car park on left. Straight, not left, at road junction well beyond village keeping on Church Road and then turn left at next road junction (SP - *Corton Denham*).

(B) At T-junction below hill go almost straight across, onto path ahead between hedges (SP - *Stafford's Green*) and soon through gate. Bear right and up around hill slope along a narrow grassy hollow. Good views backwards from top of rise, to Cadbury Castle earthworks with their grassy summit and wooded fringe. Bear left through gate into next field and follow line of fence and hawthorn trees on left. Sutton Montis, *'the village south of the mount'*, visible to right. We shall now follow crest of Corton Ridge for over a mile. Go through stile beside gate into next field with fine views to right, across broad Yeo valley and later also to left, over low stone wall towards green rounded hills - the Beacon and Corton Hill, with village of Corton Denham, nestling between the two ridges. Keep field boundary to left, go through gate into next field and keep alongside wire fence and scrubby trees.

(C) Bear left through field gates into Ridge Lane, but continue southwards by immediately turning right into field keeping hedge on left. Through three gates into next fields, still keeping hedge on left. (At third gate, route now runs just inside county of Dorset - note Dorset CC waymarks.) Through small wooden gate onto bridleway between high hedges.

(D) Soon turn left into grassy lane with tall hedges on either side. As this drops into valley, lane becomes stony track and then tarmac road. Enter hamlet of Stafford's Green at bottom of hill and almost immediately go to right, through large gate into farmyard opposite small garage of house on left. Go straight ahead between two barrel-roofed barns leaving hard surface. Continue straight ahead to go over stile beside metal gate. Just beyond stile turn half right to go over sleeper bridge. Turn left immediately beyond bridge and continue across field with hedge on right and stream on left.

Cadbury Castle from the south

(E) Gradually veer away from hedge on right and aim for far left corner of field, but at about 50 yards before stile in cross-hedge, bear left to go over sleeper bridge. Up bank beyond stream and immediately turn right to soon go over double stile. Cross long, park-like field with slopes up to left and stream down to right. Initially follow to immediate left of trees and bushes and, when Sandford Orcas Manor is visible ahead, veer slightly left following well used path. Lovely views of manor and church over to right. Beyond brow, aim for middle of

Sandford Orcas village's roof tops, stile not visible until just short of it.

(F) Over stile opposite *The Old House* and turn left onto road in Sandford Orcas *(but turn right if you wish to visit church). This quiet stone and thatch village below the hills takes the second half of its name, Orcas, from that of the Norman family of 'de Orescuily'. Its church, beautifully situated beside the manor house, has a partly restored interior containing attractive angel corbel figures, a little 13th-century font and a family chapel in its south side with an old linenfold screen and several interesting monuments. There is the base of an old cross in the churchyard, close to a fine gateway to the manor house. This delightful Ham Hill stone Tudor building (sometimes open) has fine panelling, furniture and pictures within and terraced gardens with topiary without.* Almost immediately go straight, not right (SP - Sherborne), then straight, not left (SP - Sherborne), pass phone box on right and Mitre Inn beyond on right. Walk with care through village along its narrow and quite dangerous lane, which is lined with stone cottages and pretty gardens and which winds south-east and then south for over half-a-mile.

(G) Turn left onto small surfaced lane by post box on left and *No Through Road* sign. Go up lane for 20 yards and through opening into field on left. Keeping hedge on right, cross field to gate. Through gate and go straight ahead across field, bearing slightly left, to another gate. Through gate and turn right along farm track with hedge on right. At end of hedge go past waymarked post and continue in same line to stile on edge of wood. Over stile into wood following path bending first to left and then immediately right, up a short, steep slope onto forest track. Turn left onto track and follow it up hill. Track soon becomes path through bracken and nettles. Keep straight on and emerge onto golf course. Keep close to fence and hedge on left and continue until level with clubhouse. *Fine views from here, back (north) to Glastonbury Tor and the Mendips.* Squeeze between clubhouse buildings and hedge on left.

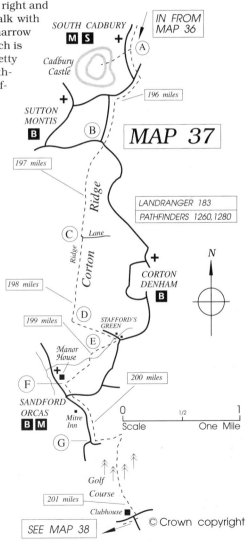

IN FROM
MAP 36

SOUTH CADBURY

Ⓜ Ⓢ ✛ Ⓐ

Cadbury
Castle

196 miles

✛

SUTTON
MONTIS

🅱 Ⓑ

MAP 37

197 miles

LANDRANGER 183
PATHFINDERS 1260, 1280

Ⓒ Lane

✛
CORTON
DENHAM
🅱

N

198 miles

Corton Ridge

Ⓓ STAFFORD'S
GREEN

199 miles

Ⓔ

Manor
House

✛ ■

Ⓕ

SANDFORD
ORCAS
🅱 Ⓜ Mitre ■
Inn

Ⓖ

200 miles

0   1/2   1
Scale   One Mile

Golf

Course

201 miles

Clubhouse ■

© Crown copyright

SEE MAP 38

(A) Pass through clubhouse gate and turn right onto road. *Good views southwards to Woolland Hill and Bulbarrow Hill, with its masts.* Turn left at T-junction of roads (SP - *Sherborne*). Down road with strip lynchets (ancient cultivation terraces) visible on hillside to right.

(B) After half-a-mile, turn left beneath beech tree onto possibly obscured track known as Quarr Lane. Follow track, overhung with trees as it climbs, but turn left where it meets hedge at what looks like T-junction of paths. Continue up hill between hedges and after curious twists and turns, track becomes more purposeful and runs down hill in south-easterly direction. *Linger at second gate on right for panoramic view of Sherborne and hills beyond.* Quarr Lane's surface changes to tarmac and then becomes a road.

(C) Now enter outskirts of Sherborne, passing bungalows on left with well-kept gardens, and further beyond on right, a large depression, once a quarry, the source of much of old Sherborne's stone (hence 'Quarr Lane'). At Mermaid Hotel avoid road which runs past it (Blackberry Lane) and go half left, to immediate left of Mermaid Cottage, to join B3145, Bristol Road. Follow this down hill to traffic lights on the busy A30. **Do not try to cross here**, but bear right onto A30 and use pedestrian crossing just along to right, opposite Antelope Hotel.

(D) Having crossed A30, bear left down Higher Cheap Street. Continue down hill, bearing left into Cheap Street by White Hart. **Take care here as Cheap Street has one-way traffic coming down hill from behind you on both sides of road.**

Sherborne is perhaps the most beautiful of all Dorset towns, so do take time off to explore its wealth of old buildings from every period. The Abbey, in the very heart of the town, was founded in AD705 by King Ine of Wessex. Visually the present building dates from the 15th century, following a disastrous fire in 1437, although it incorporates much of the Norman church built by Bishop Roger of Caen in about 1120. Sherborne Old Castle, to the east of the town, was also the work of Bishop Roger, but

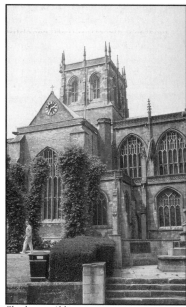

like so many other English castles, it was largely destroyed during the Civil War. All that remains is the Norman gatehouse and portions of the keep, chapel and curtain walls. The nearby, 'new' Sherborne Castle, first built by Sir Walter Raleigh in 1594, contains fine furniture, porcelain and pictures and stands beside a lake in a 20-acre park landscaped by Capability Brown.

Pass archway on left leading to supermarket. Pass Post Office with phones on left, then archway on left leading to Swan Yard and toilets. On right at lower end of Cheap Street pavement broadens to form 'The Parade', where 'The Conduit' stands. *This is an hexagonal 16th-century building which originally stood in the cloisters on the north side of the Abbey, where it served as a washing place for the monks. It was moved to its present site after the dissolution of Sherborne's monastery in 1539. This is* probably the best access point for the Abbey, just beyond.

Sherborne Abbey

(E) A short way past the Conduit follow road round to right (westwards) where it becomes Half Moon Street. *But turn left up Long Street if you wish to visit Sherborne Old Castle and Sherborne Castle (see above).* After 100 yards pass Abbey on right and Digby Road down to left - Tourist Information Centre visible on right of Digby Road, and Police Station on its left, with Railway Station at end. A few yards beyond entry to Digby Road follow one-way system round to left, where Half Moon Street becomes Westbury (SP - *Yeovil*) - this is opposite 15th-century St Johns Almshouses on right. Continue along Westbury to traffic island, where road joins A352, Dorchester road, coming in from right. Follow A352 (SP - *Dorchester*) as it bends to left by factory entrance on left (SP - *Dorchester*) and climbs to cross railway and River Yeo. Castle ruins just visible down valley to left.

(F) After another 200 yards turn right at X-rds **crossing A352 with very great care** to go on smaller road (SP - *Thornford*). **Great care should also be taken for next 300 yards.** After 200 yards beyond x-rds, and beyond entrance to Limekiln Farm on left, go straight, not left (SP - *Thornford*). Go on narrow pathway along left-hand side of road and after 100 yards, where road bends to right, turn left through kissing gate beside large metal gate. Go up often muddy lane with hedge on each side and over stile beside farm gate. Go half right for about 30 yards over rough ground to fence. Bear left to keep this fence on right and small copse on left and continue up hill. Into rough field beyond copse and keep fence on right as far as waymarked corner post.

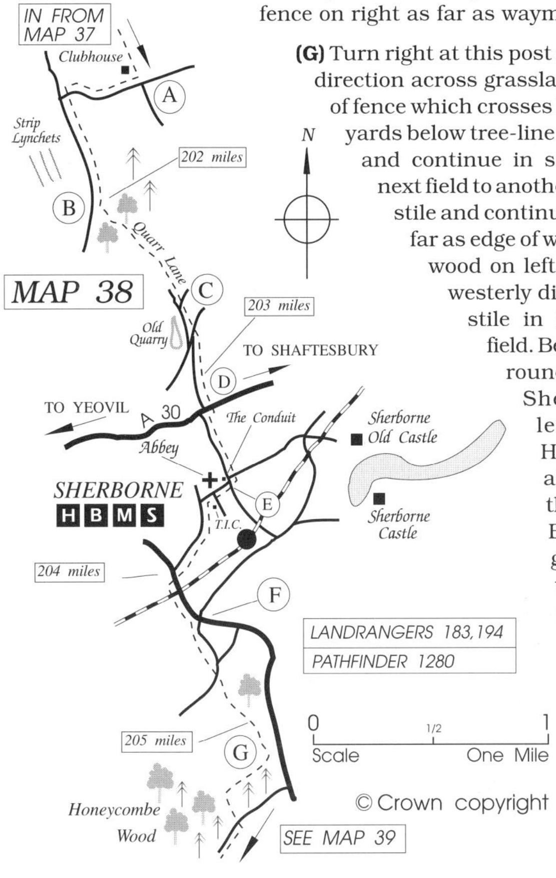

(G) Turn right at this post and head in southerly direction across grassland, aiming for middle of fence which crosses line of walk about 100 yards below tree-line. Over stile beside gate and continue in same direction across next field to another gate and stile. Cross stile and continue in same direction as far as edge of wood. Keep in field with wood on left, heading in a south-westerly direction until reaching stile in far, upper corner of field. Before crossing stile turn round to take last look at Sherborne. Over stile leading directly into Honeycombe Wood and after about 20 yards, through old wicket gate. Bear left onto track and go almost due south, up hill through wood, and shortly emerge onto road. *Opposite, on other side of road, is a gate with fine view of central Dorset, with the masts on the skyline identifying Bulbarrow Hill, eleven miles to the south-east.*

IN FROM MAP 37

Clubhouse

A

Strip Lynchets

202 miles

B

N

Quarr Lane

MAP 38

C

203 miles

Old Quarry

TO SHAFTESBURY

D

TO YEOVIL

A 30

The Conduit

Sherborne Old Castle

Abbey

SHERBORNE

H B M S

E

T.I.C.

Sherborne Castle

204 miles

F

LANDRANGERS 183,194
PATHFINDER 1280

205 miles

G

0   1/2   1
Scale   One Mile

© Crown copyright

SEE MAP 39

Honeycombe Wood

(A) Turn right beyond wood and follow minor road south-westwards with care. This is not busy but has many blind bends and, as usual, it is best to walk on outside of all bends. After almost three-quarters-of-a-mile, turn sharp left at road junction (SP - *Lillington*). At bottom of hill, in small village of Lillington, bear round to right. *But turn left if you wish to visit the largely 13th- and 15th-century church with its sympathetically restored interior.* Pass fine stone barn and phone box on left.

(B) After about 500 yards reach grassy triangle where road turns sharply right up hill. Ignore this, cross triangle and continue southwards along track bordered by high hedges. On reaching large oak tree on left, turn round to enjoy pleasant glimpse of Lillington Church. A little further on, where hedge ends, go through gate on right and aim diagonally right (south-westwards) for top left-hand corner of field, aiming for large solitary oak tree on skyline. Just before corner, at highest point of field, over stile on right in wide hedge, over sleeper bridge and second stile. (Caution: between these two stiles is deep ditch bridged by single sleeper, which may sometimes be concealed by dense undergrowth). Now aim half-left across field for stile a few yards to right of aforesaid oak tree, still dominating skyline. Cross stile (hopefully now re-built) and aim for gap in opposite hedge between willow to left and oak to right. Cross two stiles in this gap and continue in same direction aiming slightly to left of far corner of field, although gate not yet visible, being initially hidden by corner of hedge to left.

(C) Go through gate and turn right onto road (disregarding waymark pointing down road to left). Go along and up road for 400 yards and turn left immediately beyond Higher Knighton Farm on left and over stile. *Now entering the eastern fringes of Blackmoor Vale, which was named `The Vale of the Little Dairies' by the great Dorset novelist, Thomas Hardy. There is much rich pasture country to be crossed before we reach the coast, although today there are fewer milking herds and more beef cattle to be seen.* Down across small field, through or over gate and go diagonally right across next field to gate. Through or over gate and go diagonally right, across field aiming to right of single tree.

(D) Beyond tree go through gate to cross minor road known as Knighton Lane and through gate opposite. Around tip of wood on right known as Tibbles Copse and veer slightly to left, heading south-westerly for gate. Through gate and over farm bridge crossing stream and go diagonally left across field aiming for double-stile to left of

single tree in hedge. Over double-stile and go slightly left following waymark direction across field and aiming for metal gate to left of two trees in field. Through gate and across field to another gate in hedge.

(E) Through large gate to right of water-trough and go diagonally right across field aiming slightly to left of Yetminster church (just visible on skyline ahead). Go through another gate to left of metal water-trough and cross corner of field aiming for gate in side hedge with feed silo beyond. Through metal gate and along left-hand edge of field with farm building just beyond hedge. Cross exit lane from Westfield Farm buildings on left. Continue to stile with sleeper across possible mud patch beyond. Cross field to stile in opposite hedge and into Yetminster playing-fields. Follow hedge, going behind sports pavilion and then go down drive past allotments and small housing estate before

Lillington from the south

84

Some of Yetminster's delightful old houses

turning right onto road just to left of railway bridge in Brister End, Yetminster.

(F) Over railway bridge and bear left to continue towards Yetminster centre, with railway station and Railway Inn to right. *Yetminster is a large village lying in low country and possessing a wealth of interesting old houses, of which no fewer than 31 are 'listed buildings'. The tall tower of the handsome 13th- to 15th-century church has some fine gargoyles and a golden weathercock. Its bright interior is full of interest, with painted wagon-roof, 16th-century benches, a Norman font and some good monuments. Benjamin Jesty, probably the first man to vaccinate using cowpox, lived here in the 18th century and his descendants still live locally. More recently the Yetties Folk Group were all born here and still often play at village occasions.* Pass Manor Farm Guest House on right and turn left at triangle by Oak House Stores into Church Street (but go straight ahead up High Street if you wish to visit Post Office, telephone box, rest of useful shops or White Hart Inn). Pass Old School and Old Library on left, new Rectory, Village Hall and church on right. *Just beyond church is Sexton's Cottage, dated 1736. The farm on the right with large wooden gates is Upbury, oldest house in the village and once the home of Benjamin Jesty.*

(G) By clipped yew tree at junction with Mill Lane and Birch Lane, take path to left of tree and through kissing gate. Go diagonally right, across field to stile in high hedge. Down steps onto road, turn left and continue southwards down hill **with great care**, to go straight across at road junction (SP - *Melbury Osmond*). Through next gate on left and turn right to continue in same line, parallel with road. Over possible electric fence where field narrows, start to cross to left-hand hedge and follow it to metal gate and stile in field corner.

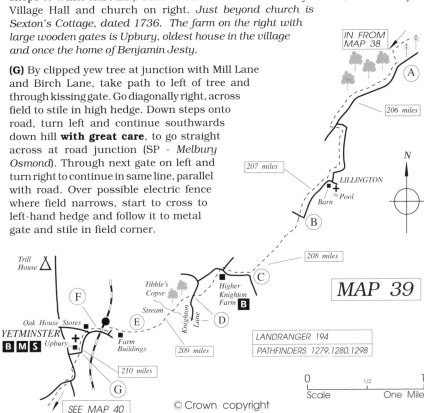

IN FROM MAP 38

206 miles

207 miles

N

LILLINGTON
Barn · Pool
B

208 miles

Trill House

Tibble's Copse

Higher Knighton Farm **B**

F

Stream

Knighton Lane

E

D

Oak House Stores
YETMINSTER
B **M** **S** Upbury
Farm Buildings

209 miles

210 miles

G

MAP 39

LANDRANGER 194
PATHFINDERS 1279, 1280, 1298

0   1/2   1
Scale   One Mile

SEE MAP 40

© Crown copyright

(A) Over stile and cross sometimes wet and muddy Horsehill Lane, to go slightly left to search for, and go over, half-hidden sleeper bridge and stile. Beyond stile follow left-hand hedge for short distance to cross field hedge to high stile. Over this stile and go between hedge and roped-off field to right (livery stables over to right). At next cross-hedge, over two sleepers and stiles in quick succession. After stiles go left to cut corner of field, going to left-hand hedge to cross a double-stile. Now go diagonally left to cross large, long field to hedge, soon going to left-hand edge of field (which runs south-eastwards) and follow this to stile below and to immediate right of large oak tree. Over stile and keep to right of hedge. Keep between bushes and hedge to possibly tied-up gate.

(B) Through gate and turn right into Woodville Lane, rutted and sometimes muddy, but delightful in high summer, with overhanging trees and bushes. Where lane turns sharp right, go straight ahead through gate and follow waymark direction all along right-hand hedge, but cut left across far corner of field and go through old metal gate in hedge. Take short path to lane. Turn left here, onto stony path and bridge-like, concrete-covered drain, to new gate at end of lane. Through new gate and turn diagonally left to head almost due south for wooded edge of field. Follow field edge of large wood, known as Chetnole Withy Bed, aiming for single oak tree outside wood with barbed wire fence on left forming boundary of what was once a lane. Follow fence as closely as possible to far left-hand (south-west) corner of wood where lane becomes obvious, to gate where lane turns left (east) through possibly boggy area into wood.

(C) Through this gate and along lush green-lane which runs within copse, until turning right (south) through old metal gate into field. Traces of lane have vanished, although this was once known as Starveacre Lane. Follow hedge on left to cross-field hedge, and just before reaching this gated hedge, ignore stile to left. Go ahead through metal gate and continue to follow hedge and ditch on left until reaching another cross-hedge. Turn right and after a few yards go left through wide gap into remains of old lane. Turn right and enter drove-road (sliding poles here) ignoring farm lane going south to Manor Farm. Continue along drove-road which eventually opens out. Keep to left-hand corner to cross narrow stream. This is fordable, but it is often muddy. Go into field through gap and continue south-westwards with hedge on left. Leave field through old metal gate and into car park of Welcome Inn.

(D) Cross busy A37 with great care and turn right to walk northwards along verge for 100 yards. *But go a further 100 yards beyond if you wish to visit The Oak House (B & B).* Turn left, go over fence, along field edge with hedge on left for about 200 yards and then go downhill across field to right-hand corner keeping to left of farm buildings. Over stile and turn right onto estate drive. Turn left onto road in Drive End and follow road westwards, eventually going over two flat bridges. Just before

second thatched cottage on left through gate on left, following tarmac path to The Meads, a lane leading to Melbury Osmond village street south of the church. *Melbury Osmond is a delightful stone and thatch village, very much part of the great Ilchester Estate (see below). The ill-fated Duke of Monmouth is reputed to have stopped here, the cottage in question being named after him. Thomas Hardy re-named the village* King's Hintock *in*

Our entry to Melbury Park

86

his novels and it was in St Osmond's Church that both his grandparents and his parents were married. At that time the church must have had a pleasant Georgian appearance, but it was thoroughly 'restored' in 1888 and its only really noteworthy feature is a strange 10th- or 11th-century stone carving which may represent 'Abraham's ram caught in a thicket'.

(E) Turn left onto village street (but turn right to visit church or use telephone box or bus shelter). Go past attractive watersplash and along road to Town's End. Pass Monmouth Cottage on left and follow road to gates of Melbury Park. Turn right here into small picnic area and then over stile onto estate drive. Follow this drive southwards through parkland for about three-quarters-of-a-mile to Melbury House.

(F) Turn right following drive around right-hand side of Melbury House and then south again through further delightful parkland. *The principal seat of the Fox-Strangways family, the Earls of Ilchester, Melbury House, together with the adjoining church, makes up the 'village' of Melbury Sampford, which is situated in the large and very beautiful deer park through which we are walking. The massive, rambling house (not open to visitors) was built by Giles Strangways in the 16th century but has been considerably altered and added to in the 17th and 19th centuries. The fine Tudor hexagonal tower, possibly intended as a point from which to observe deer hunting in the great park, is its most interesting feature. The church contains a large number of monuments commemorating members of the Strangways family and also the Brunings, the earlier occupiers of Melbury Sampford.*

(G) After about a mile, leave park through main entrance and eventually pass Ilchester Estate Office on right. Now bear right onto road at entry to Evershot by triangular green known as 'The Common'. Head towards village centre passing village hall on left and Rectory House Hotel on right. *Standing at a surprising 700 feet above sea level, Evershot is Dorset's second highest village. Several bow-fronted windows look out from stone and thatch cottages across its attractive, sloping main street. The friendly Acorn Inn was renamed the 'Sow and Acorn' by Thomas Hardy in* Tess of the d'Urbervilles *and in this novel Tess breakfasts at the cottage next to the church. The latter building was much restored in the 19th century.* Take next turn to left (SP - *Rampisham*) (but go straight ahead for Acorn Inn, church and phone box).

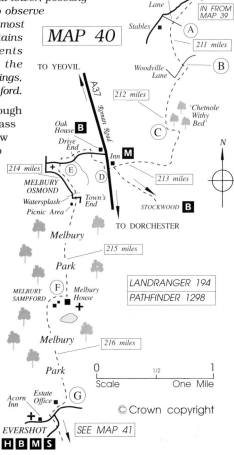

MAP 40

© Crown copyright

LANDRANGER 194
PATHFINDER 1298

SEE MAP 41

(A) Having turned first left in Evershot, pass school on left and soon turn left off road, through metal gate opposite entrance to Summer Lodge Hotel. Cross field diagonally southwards to top right-hand corner, through gate, then bear slightly left keeping hedge to immediate right (do **not** turn right through hedge). Follow hedge, cross a farm lane entrance. Keep on same line to go through gate in cross-hedge. Bear slightly left (south-east) to gate onto farm lane. Continue in same direction down lane, passing farm cottages on left, then Fortunewood Farmhouse on right and finally going left on farm lane to left of dutch barn.

(B) Towards end of barn go left through metal gate and bear right onto farm track. Follow this lane to small junction of gates and go through middle one. Continue in same direction with fence on immediate left and beyond fence's end, head for gate in field corner to right of corner of small spinney. Through this gate and aim for stile in fence beyond often boggy area with stream. Over stile and continue in same direction to left of oak tree in field corner. Bear left through metal gate into beginning of farm track. Follow this track, often wet and muddy in places, until it reaches tarmac surfaced area of what was Dorset Police Training College, Chantmarle.

(C) Turn right (south-west) at entry to Chantmarle, continue along concrete roadway past storehouse and small training tower on right and some houses on left. Bear left, up across rough ground with trees and almost immediately go through small gate below power-pole into field. Turn right cutting off corner of field and then turn left along hedge. Follow to left of this hedge with wooded hollow to left and where hedge turns sharp right, bear half-left across field aiming for right-hand end of woodlands in hollow ahead. Go through gate just within right-hand end of these woodlands and onto farm drive.

(D) Cross drive, going slightly right, to go through gate. North Holway Farm visible to left. Go almost straight across field to gate in middle of hedge. Through gate and continue in same direction across narrow corner of field and through gap in hedge with old metal fence acting as gate. Keep straight across large field and through another gap with old metal fence acting as gate into next field, turning left, then right, to go with hedge to immediate left. Follow this hedge to Holway Farm and go through right-hand of two gates keeping to right of farm buildings. Veer left at end of buildings and silage store area, to go down field to left-hand of two gates in field corner and exit at old farm lane's junction with road.

(E) Turn left (southwards) down road and turn left at road junction by grassy triangle (SP - *Cattistock*) to go over bridge across railway line, and enter hamlet of Sandhills just beyond. Keep on road through Sandhills hamlet (SP - *Cattistock*). Enter Cattistock and just beyond Post Office Stores on right and just before Fox and Hounds Inn on left, go into churchyard. *Described as 'elbow-street Cattistock' by the 19th-century Dorset poet, William Barnes, this attractive little village nestling in the upper valley of the River Frome, still has its 19th-century houses grouped around a sharp hairpin bend near the church. Most of this was rebuilt in 1857 by Sir Gilbert Scott, but the splendidly pinnacled tower was added by his son, George, in 1874. The screened-off baptistry beneath the tower, contains a font with an impressive cover, all of 20 feet high, and makes a visit here well worthwhile.*

Cattistock Church

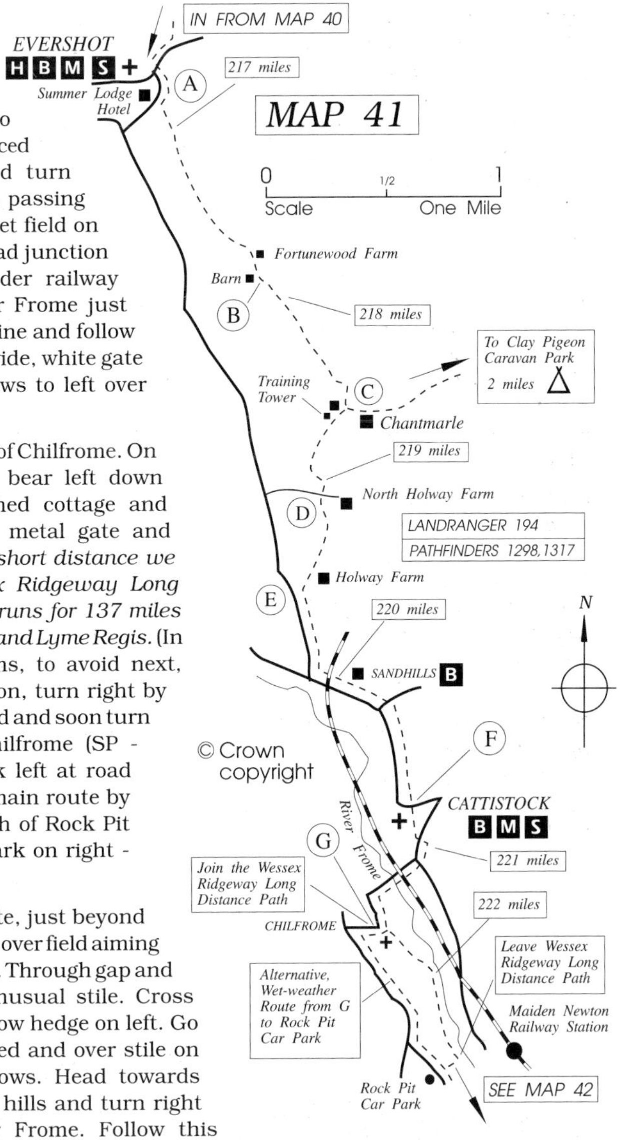

(F) Keep to left of church and follow path down to metal gate, passing ornate sunken spring down to left. Continue along fenced path southwards and turn right onto road, soon passing beautifully sited cricket field on right. Turn right at road junction (SP - Chilfrome), under railway bridge and over River Frome just beyond. Up slight incline and follow road round to left by wide, white gate on right. Pleasant views to left over valley to hills beyond.

(G) Soon enter hamlet of Chilfrome. On approaching church, bear left down track between thatched cottage and churchyard, through metal gate and into field. *For a very short distance we now join the Wessex Ridgeway Long Distance Path, which runs for 137 miles between Marlborough and Lyme Regis. (In wet-weather conditions, to avoid next, possibly flooded section, turn right by church keeping on road and soon turn left by houses in Chilfrome (SP - Maiden Newton). Fork left at road junction and re-join main route by stile on left, just north of Rock Pit Farm Walkers' Car Park on right - see page 90, Point A).*

(G) Back on main route, just beyond Chilfrome Church - Go over field aiming for gap in hedge ahead. Through gap and cross next field to unusual stile. Cross stile, turn left and follow hedge on left. Go round crop if cultivated and over stile on left into water meadows. Head towards wooded area in lee of hills and turn right when reaching River Frome. Follow this

EVERSHOT

H B M S +

Summer Lodge ■
Hotel

IN FROM MAP 40

217 miles

Ⓐ

MAP 41

```
0                1/2            1
Scale                    One Mile
```

■ Fortunewood Farm

Barn ■

Ⓑ

218 miles

To Clay Pigeon
Caravan Park
2 miles △

Training
Tower

Ⓒ

■ Chantmarle

219 miles

Ⓓ

North Holway Farm

LANDRANGER 194
PATHFINDERS 1298, 1317

■ Holway Farm

Ⓔ

220 miles

N

■ SANDHILLS **B**

© Crown
copyright

River Frome

Ⓕ

CATTISTOCK

B M S

Ⓖ

221 miles

+

Join the Wessex
Ridgeway Long
Distance Path

CHILFROME

222 miles

Leave Wessex
Ridgeway Long
Distance Path

+

Alternative,
Wet-weather
Route from G
to Rock Pit
Car Park

Maiden Newton
Railway Station

Rock Pit ●
Car Park

SEE MAP 42

through attractive area - cool, with pleasant water-based vegetation and many different species of trees, including alder, willow, beech, ash and hazel. Go under red-brick railway arch, which carried now defunct Maiden Newton - Bridport branch line, and continue in lush vegetation. Pass buildings above on left, with several private bridges. When reaching footbridge crossing river to left, bear right *parting company with the Wessex Ridgeway Long Distance Path,* and follow permissive path on right, going slightly uphill to road. Over stile and turn left onto road opposite Rock Pit Car Park. *There are picnic tables here and an Information Board relating to the history and geology of the vicinity. During World War II, large naval guns were sited in the nearby quarries, aimed at the coast near Weymouth.*

(A) Go down road beyond Rock Pit Car Park and **go over busy A356 with great care** (but turn left if you wish to visit Maiden Newton with its bakery/general store, telephone, Post Office, inns, and railway station). On main route, next to village noticeboard, go over footbridge ahead. Bear slightly left across field to go through wooden gate in corner. Follow path beside River Frome until reaching metal gate on left. Through gate and turn right onto lane.

(B) Soon turn right (SP - *Cruxton*) near Frome Vauchurch church (which is ahead on left). *The small church here was much restored in 1870, but some of its Norman and Early English features were retained and its contents include a Jacobean pulpit. There are also pleasant old tabletop tombs in its little tree-shaded churchyard.* Soon turn left at next road junction (SP - *Cruxton*).

(C) Through Cruxton hamlet where tarmac road becomes track. Follow track uphill through field (SP - *Notton*). Follow sign on right directing us left. Soon turn right (SP - *Compton Valence*) and go on concrete roadway (with hedge on right) which eventually becomes unsurfaced track. At top of hill do **not** go through fenced opening (single wire) ahead, but turn left and after few yards turn right through opening in hedge. Continue across long field with hedge on immediate right and at corner, where there is a modern wooden sign, turn left still keeping hedge on right. Over stile in corner of field and bear right, downhill, across grass field towards now visible Notton Hill Barn.

(D) Aim for gate to left of Notton Hill Barn complex, go through this gate and turn right down lane past buildings on right. Through two metal gates, down one slope and up the next, with attractive open views on both sides. Continue to end of furthest field on ridge with hedge on right - the last part of this route is on grass - do **not** follow any track to right. When reaching corner of field note three gates on right and wooden sign. Go through all three and turn left (SP - *Compton Valence*). With hedge now on left continue down slope on grassy track towards Compton Bottom. Compton Valence now visible ahead. Go through metal gate bearing right along track with beautiful views of green and unspoilt valley. Keep following track which bears sharp right. On reaching valley floor with its badger sets, go through gate where two fences on left meet at right-angles. Continue down green slope across field, bearing right of solitary tree.

(E) Keep bearing right, go through gate in corner of field and turn right onto well defined track. Soon pass farm buildings and converted barns before emerging onto road in minute village of C o m p t o n Valence. Turn right, past phone box on right and then turn left opposite small Victorian church onto surfaced l a n e (**N o t** through gate to its right into

Downland track to Compton Valence

90

woods). Go along and then up lane through pleasant woodlands of Compton Valence House, with attractive gardens and pond on right. Follow lane round to right and by small garage-like building on left, carry straight ahead and up through metal gate where lane bears to left. Go up pleasant, shaded green lane.

(F) At top of hill, after passing small partly obstructed area, bear left into field. Now continue southwards, with hedge on immediate left. Attractive views to left down into dry valley. Go over stile at end of field and turn left to go down minor road which follows course of possible Roman Road. After about 50 yards, turn right off road, through first metal gate and immediately through gap in hedge to left. Go along field keeping to immediate left of hedge-line. Cross over wooden fence in next hedge-line into large meadow. Go downhill keeping to left of hedge, then up again and under high-voltage power-line.

(G) *At this point we cross a bridleway carrying the Dorset Jubilee Trail, a 90-mile regional path running westwards across the county from Forde Abbey to Bokerley Dyke, between Blandford and Salisbury.* Good views ahead of ridge beyond Bride Valley, with Hardy Monument clearly visible on left (in memory of Admiral Hardy, Nelson's 'Captain Hardy' at Trafalgar). Carry on southwards, through metal gate, to clump of trees ahead. Follow track downwards to Kingston Russell Farm, joining lane through farmyard and then forking right along surfaced lane to A35. **Cross very busy A35 with great care** and through metal hunting gate to right of concrete farm road and onto this farm road to go gently up hill.

(H) Turn left by storage pit on right and, if possible, follow to immediate left of fence-line. Through hunting gate below small, wind-bent hawthorn tree and immediately turn right. *Note to left of hawthorn tree, small round-barrow topped by a boulder - probably part of its original burial chamber. Lovely pastoral views over Bride Valley ahead and to ridge in distance beyond.*

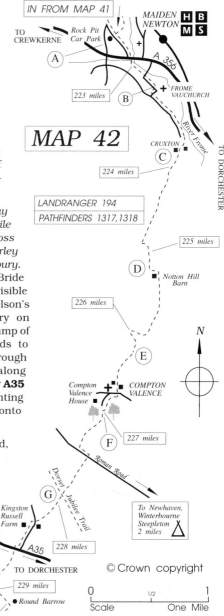

IN FROM MAP 41

MAIDEN NEWTON [H][B][M][S]

TO CREWKERNE

Rock Pit Car Park

A 356

FROME VAUCHURCH

River Frome

TO DORCHESTER

A

223 miles

B

MAP 42

CRUXTON

C

224 miles

LANDRANGER 194

PATHFINDERS 1317,1318

225 miles

D

Notton Hill Barn

226 miles

N

E

Compton Valence House

COMPTON VALENCE

227 miles

F

Roman Road

To Newhaven, Winterbourne Steepleton 2 miles

Dorset Jubilee Trail

G

Kingston Russell Farm

TO BRIDPORT

A35

228 miles

H

TO DORCHESTER

Storage Pit

229 miles

SEE MAP 43

Round Barrow

0   1/2   1
Scale   One Mile

(A) Go through metal gate with wire fence on right (SP - *Bridleway to Whatcombe*) and down pleasant sunken lane with, in high summer, many butterflies and the scent of camomile. Beware of deep rutts in track. *Kingston Russell House visible ahead right. This elegant 16th- and 18th-century house stands on the site of what was once the home of the forbears of the Dukes of Bedford.* Thick hedge to right, but pleasant views to left of ridges and grassy downland.

(B) Through metal gate at bottom of hill and cross minor road with care, in view of sharp left-hand bend just to right. *But if conditions have been very wet, turn right onto road, turn left at T-junction in Long Bredy, go straight, not left at next junction, turn left at Lower Farm and go down farm road to rejoin main route at Point C, by turning right.* However in dry weather stay on main route by going straight across road, through metal gate onto what may seem an overgrown path but which, with care, is quite passable. Path eventually narrows and brambles and nettles may cause problems but there is campion to compensate. Hedges on both sides soon become thicker and taller, and path appears to follow bed of stream. Kingston Russell House lies beyond thick hedge on right. Despair not if things seem jungly as path suddenly emerges into pleasant, small grassy meadow. Bear round to right and through gate with house on right. Then turn left, over footbridge beside ford across little River Bride and along well surfaced drive.

(C) Go through drive's gate and up road ahead. *We are joined here by wet-weather alternative coming in from right.* Three telegraph poles on, where a track goes **sharp**-left, go **half**-left through rusty metal gate into field. Head diagonally across field passing power-pole, going over insulated fence and through gate bearing right. Good views back to ridge, with Whatcombe House prominent on hill to right. Keep in lee of wood on right and then turn right through hunting gate on right. Traverse wood (path often boggy - possibly go parallel, slightly to right of path) and soon emerge into field with more pastoral views. Continue in same direction across field

and through wooden gate. Ignoring track to left, go ahead slightly uphill, through metal gate and after looking to right to distant view of Lyme Bay (the sea at last!), head for next gate, which has a venerable sycamore tree behind it.

(D) Go through gate and bear diagonally left up well-defined track. Pass thin hedge of tall hawthorn trees on left and then turn left through movable wire fence (known locally as a 'Hampshire Gate') and under barbed-wire beyond into next field. Continue in same direction diagonally across next field (Tenants Hill) and over brow to its far corner where stands the Kingston Russell Stone Circle (sometimes partly hidden by growing crop). *This Bronze Age stone circle has 18 low stones and stands at a point where no fewer than five public footpaths converge. It is described on an English Heritage information board and there are splendid all-round views.*

Track down to Kingston Russell

(E) Go through **metal** gate on right, in corner of field just beyond stone circle, and follow to immediate right of hedge-line, going south-westwards. Through next gate and note attractive view of valley and, to right, the sea below Golden Cap, some miles to west, beyond Bridport. Continue downhill towards wooded area on left. Go through metal gate, bear right, round back of cottages and then left through gate onto lane. Go past cottages, through Gorwell Farm and along surfaced road through pleasant wooded area.

(F) At end of wooded area on right, where private road bears left, turn right to go up hill along concrete path with hedge on right. Pass first metal gate where concrete path becomes track and then, after short distance, go through second metal gate. Now bear slightly right across open field eventually joining remains of grassy track. *Soon come to highest point of rounded White Hill, with its splendid views over Abbotsbury to the sea, including the long line of Chesil Bank with the lagoons of the Fleet on its landward side, and the peninsula of Portland Bill beyond to the east.*

(G) Go down hill and over stile in fence to left of signpost indicating inland alternative of South-West Coastal Path, which we cross. Now on limestone terrace, part of old quarry workings and a good place to stop awhile. *The limestone in the quarries is part of the same family group of oolite over which the Macmillan Way has been passing since its start at Oakham some 230 miles to the north-east. Much of the village of Abbotsbury still lies hidden below and beyond the brow, but the very satisfying view covers, from right - White Nothe Cliff, Weymouth Bay, Isle of Portland, Chesil Bank, the Fleet, and directly ahead, in the near distance - the Swannery, St Catherine's Chapel and just below it, Abbotsbury's church and tithe barn.* Now go through metal gate to left. Pass signpost to Abbotsbury and an interesting notice regarding old quarry workings and continue down hill with Abbotsbury coming into view. Go through metal gate and follow track bearing left and noting strip lynchets just ahead to right. Continue down hill passing signpost to Abbotsbury on left and through metal gate into grassy, rocky lane (very slippery in wet weather). Lane narrows to a path and drops steeply, going round to left, then right into Abbotsbury village.

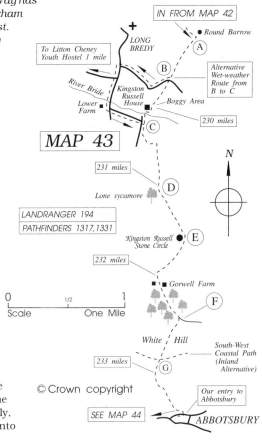

IN FROM MAP 42

Round Barrow

LONG BREDY

To Litton Cheney Youth Hostel 1 mile

A

B

Alternative Wet-weather Route from B to C

River Bride

Kingston Russell House

Lower Farm

Boggy Area

230 miles

C

MAP 43

N

231 miles

Lone sycamore

D

LANDRANGER 194

PATHFINDERS 1317, 1331

Kingston Russell Stone Circle

E

232 miles

Gorwell Farm

0   1/2   1

Scale   One Mile

F

White   Hill

South-West Coastal Path (Inland Alternative)

233 miles

G

© Crown copyright

Our entry to Abbotsbury

SEE MAP 44

ABBOTSBURY

Abbotsbury *is an unspoilt stone and thatch village amidst partly wooded downland country just inland from the sea, where Chesil Beach joins the mainland. Its Benedictine Abbey was founded in the 11th century by Orc, King Canute's chief steward and flourished for 500 years before being largely demolished following the Dissolution of the Monasteries in 1539. The remaining ruins are not over-exciting, but the splendid 14th-century tithe barn, which now contains a museum devoted mainly to agricultural bygones, is well worth visiting. The nearby parish church is also full of interest, including an unusual plastered and barrel-vaulted chancel ceiling and a fine Jacobean pulpit. Standing by itself on a little hill just to the south-west of the village, and on our route, is the little St Catherine's Chapel. Also barrel-vaulted and stoutly buttressed, this was built by the monks of Abbotsbury in the 14th century as a landmark for sailors. On the shore of the Fleet, almost due south of St Catherine's, is Abbotsbury's best known feature - The Swannery. First mentioned as early as 1393, it has, like the rest of Abbotsbury, been in the hands of the Strangways family since the Dissolution. The swans stay here because there is a plentiful supply of their favourite food growing in the Fleet, a type of seaweed known as Zostera Marina. In sheltering woods well to the west of the village are Abbotsbury's other well known feature - The Sub-Tropical Gardens, which are possibly best visited after your conclusion of the Macmillan Way (see below). Originally laid out in the 18th century, these gardens are well sheltered from the sea and usually frost-free. Consequently many exotic plants are to be found here, in addition to palms, bamboos, camellias, rhododendrons and azaleas.*

(H) Turn right onto minor road in Abbotsbury and, just beyond phone box on right, bear right onto B3157 by Post Office and Ilchester Arms, keeping in same, westerly direction (but turn left if you wish to visit Church, Tithe Barn or Swannery). Cross to south side of road and turn left at first lane (sign - *St Catherine's Chapel*), between pottery and Chapel Lane Stores. This shop is almost always open and it is hoped that you will call in to record your completion of the Macmillan Way (or of part of it) in the Record Book kept here. It is hoped to have badges and other mementoes on sale here and it will be possible to arrange for a certificate recording your achievement to be sent to you. This lane soon becomes a track and St Catherine's Chapel is visible on hill to right. Go through metal gate (SP - *St Catherine's Chapel*) and follow track up hill to St Catherine's Chapel.

(J) After visiting chapel drop down south-eastwards following permissive path over open field. Over stile with copse on left until reaching stone sign on cross-track, which is southern option of South-West Coastal Path. Turn right and follow South-West Coast Path's track to reach stile (SP - *Tropical Gardens*). Over stile and bear left, following South-West Coastal Path. Chesil Beach is now ahead but path bears round to right and in just over half-a-mile arrive at Chesil Beach Car Park (Toilets).

(K) Go up and over the Chesil Beach on wooden footway to arrive at the sea-shore - and the end of your 235-mile-long journey along the Macmillan Way from the heart of England at Oakham.

Congratulations on completing your journey. We hope that you have enjoyed it all. If you have been unable to call at the Chapel Lane Stores in Abbotsbury, but would like a Certificate to record

Abbotsbury Tithe Barn

St Catherine's Chapel, Abbotsbury

your achievement, please write to us - *The Macmillan Way Association, St Mary's Barn, Pillerton Priors, Warwick CV35 0PG.* **If, at the same time, you feel like making a small contribution to the Cancer Relief Macmillan Fund, for the support of which the Macmillan Way was both established and continues to be maintained, it would be much appreciated.** Your contribution will be forwarded to them without any deduction and your generosity and that of any possible sponsoring friends and relations, will be recorded on the certificate which you will receive. See page 5 for further details.

We should also be most interested to hear how you fared, so do drop us a line if you can spare a few moments. If, on the other hand, you are already setting out from Abbotsbury to Land's End on the South-West Coast Path, we shall not expect to hear from you for a week or so ! But whatever your next objective - Good Luck and Happy Walking.

MAP 44

NOTE: THIS MAP IS TWICE THE NORMAL SCALE

LANDRANGER 194
PATHFINDER 1331

Chapel Lane Stores
Check-in Point

IN FROM
MAP 43

Ⓐ

ABBOTSBURY
H M B S

235 miles

Abbotsbury
Sub-Tropical
Gardens

South-West Coast Path

South-West
Coast Path
to Minehead

234 miles

St Catherine's
Chapel

Ⓑ

Abbey
Ruins

Tithe Barn
(Museum)

To Portesham
Dairy
Farm
2 miles

South-West
Coast Path
to Poole

Ⓒ

Car Park
and Toilets

N

Chesil Beach

Journey's End
. . 235 miles
from Oakham

Abbotsbury
Swannery

To Camp Sites at
Langton Herring,
Fleet, Bagwell
and Chickerell.
Between 3
and 6 miles

The Fleet
(part of)

0 ————— 1/2
Scale   Half-a-Mile

© Crown
copyright

INDEX

Abbotsbury 93,94,95
Abbotsbury Swannery 94
Adlestrop 38
Alfred's Tower 72-73
Alkerton 32
Allexton 10
Althorp Park 20
Ascott 34
Aston Blank 42
Avening 51-52
Avoncliff 64
Beckington 66
Belton-in-Rutland 9
Beverston 53
Blue Vein 61
Bourton-on-the-Water 41
Box 60-61
Bradford-on-Avon 63-64
Brampton Ash 14
Brampton Valley Way 16-17
Braybrooke 14-15
Brington, Great 20
Brington, Little 20
Brook End 55
Brooke 8
Bruton 75-76
Buckland Dinham 68
Buckle Street 41
Cadbury, North 78-79
Cadbury, South 79
Cadbury Castle 80
Canons Ashby 25
Castle Cary 77
Castle Combe 58
Cattistock 88-89
Centenary Way 30
Chantmarle 88
Chapel Cross 79
Chastleton 37
Chavenage House 52
Chedworth 45
Chedworth Roman Villa 44-45
Cherington 51
Chilfrome 89
Chipping Warden 27
Church Stowe 23
Cirencester 46
Cirencester Park 48-49
Claydon 28
Coates 50
Cold Aston 42
Cole 76
Compton Valence 90-91
Cottesbrooke 18
Creaton 18
Cruxton 90
Daylesford 39
Ditchedge Lane 34
Dorset Jubilee Trail 91
Druly Hill Farm 72

Duntisbourne Rouse 47-48
d'Arcy Dalton Way 32
East Mendip Way 69
Edge Hill 31
Edgehill, Battle of 31
Epwell 33
Ermin Way 47
Evershot 87-88
Eydon 26
Farleigh Hungerford 64,65
Farnborough 28-29
Farnborough Hall 29
Farthingstone 23-24
Flore 21-22
Ford 59
Fosse Way 40, 57
Frome Vauchurch 90
Gatcombe Park 52
Granary Museum of Bygones 28
Grand Union Canal Path 22
Great Brington 20
Great Elm 68-69
Great Oxendon 16
Hallaton 11
Hampnett 43
Hangman's Stone 44
Hazleton Manor 50
Heart of England Way 40
Henley 61
Higher Knighton 84
Highgrove House 52
Holdenby 19-20
Iford Manor 64
Jurassic Way 14,16,27
Kennet & Avon Canal Path 64
Kingston Russell Farm 91
Kingston Russell House 92
Kingston Russell Stone Circle 92
Leland Trail 72-73, 78-79
Lillington 84
Little Brington 21
Littleton Drew 57
Long Bredy 92
Long Compton 35-36
Long Dean 58
Lower Slaughter 40-41
Luckington 56
Lugbury Long Barrow 56,57
Lullington 67
Macmillan, Douglas 6,75,76,77
Macmillan Way Planner 5
Yetminster 85
Maiden Newton 90
Maidwell 17
Market Harborough 15
Maugersbury 39
Medbourne 12
Melbury Osmond 86-87
Melbury Sampford 87
Mells 69
Midshires Way 13
Moreton Pinkney 25-26
Nene Way 22

Nettleton Mill 57
North Cadbury 78-79
Northleach 43
Nunney 70
Oakham 8
Oddington 38-39
Old Coach Road 74
Orchardleigh Park 67
Oxford Canal 28
Pinbury Park 48
Ratley 30
Redlynch Park 74
Rendcomb 46
Rock Pit Car Park 89-90
Rode 66
Rollright Stones 36
Sandford Orcas 80-81
Sandhills 88
Sapperton 48
Shenington 32
Sherborne 82-83
Sherston 54-55
Silk Wood, The 54
Slaughterford 59
South Cadbury 79
South Wraxall 62
St Catherine's Chapel 94
Stourhead 73
Stow-on-the-Wold 39-40
Sunrising Hill 31
Tarlton 50
Teeton 18
Tellisford 65
Tetbury 52
Thames Head 50
Thames Path 50
Thames & Severn Canal 48,49
Traitor's Ford 34
Trudoxhill 70
Tunnel House Inn 49-50
Turkdean 42
Upton House 31
Vale of Red Horse 31
Wardens' Way 41
Warmington 29-30
Weedon Bec 22
Wessex Ridgeway Path 89
Weston by Welland 12
Westonbirt Arboretum 54
Westwood 64
Whatley 69
Whichford 34-35
Windrush Way 41
Witham Hall Farm 70
Witham House 71
Woodmancote 47
Wyck Champflower 76
Yanworth 44

✱   ✱   ✱